Art Textiles of the World

Editor: Matthew Koumis
Copy Editor: Margie Barton
Photo Editor: Matthew Koumis and Alice Kettle
Design and typeset by Celsius, Winchester
Reprographics by Studio Technology, Leeds
Printed by Grafiche AZ, Verona, Italy

Published by
Telos Art Publishing
PO Box 125, Winchester
SO23 7UJ
telephone: ++44 (0)1962 864 546
facsimile: ++44 (0)1962 864 727
e-mail: editorial@telos.net
www.arttextiles.com

Notes: all dimensions are shown in centimetres and inches,
height x width (x depth)
Artists' biographies included within this volume have been edited to a consistent length.

Photo Credits:

Kyoung Ae Cho, Bill Bachhuber, Jon Blumb, Jeff Bruce, Jenny Carter, William
Drehfal, M. Lee Fatheree, Thibault Jeanson, Dick Kaiser, David Kingsbury, Matthew
McFarland, Dan Meyers, Cheryl O'Brien, Richard Ross, E.G. Schempf, Jimmy
Shipman, Al Surrat, Tim Thayer, John Zerbarini. Photos of Ann Hamilton's work are
reproduced with kind permission of Sean Kelly Gallery, New York.

Editor's Acknowledgements:

This book is dedicated to Poppy, Tamsin and Maia – *carpe diem!* Sincere thanks to
all those on both sides of the Atlantic and further afield who have offered advice,
assistance and encouragement, including Margie Barton; Janet De Boer at TAFTA;
Lois Borgenicht; Annet Couwenberg at the Maryland Institute; Lisa Daniel at the
bookshop of the Crafts Council; Kristen Dibbs; Edward Fennell; Shelly Goldsmith at
Winchester School of Art (University of Southampton); Maggie Grey at World of
Embroidery; Dr Jennifer Harris at the Whitworth Art Gallery (University of
Manchester); Katherine James; Janis Jefferies at Goldsmiths College (London
University); Adriana Lopez Mosqueira; Paul Markham at StudioTec; Clair O'Leary at
the Tate Modern; Paul Richardson of Oxford Brookes University; Mary Swann; Dr
Janet Summerton of the University of Sussex, Dery and Wim Timmer. Thanks to Ann
Batchelder and Nancy Orban at Fiberarts and to all at Surface Design Journal for
kind cooperation in allowing me to browse back copies of both journals. Special
thanks for their supreme patience to all ten artists, to my family and to Melanie Cook
at Celsius. I am indebted to Professor Sue Rowley (University of New South Wales,
College of Fine Arts) for the idea (p8) of a travelling international show: Her show,
Crossing Borders: Contemporary Australian Textile Art, which toured the USA in 1998,
was a collaborative project with Christopher Leitch (Kansas City Art Institute, USA)
with public and corporate sponsorship. Finally, the support of Southern Arts is
gratefully acknowledged, with thanks to David Kay.

supported
by SOUTHERN ARTS

Art Textiles of the World

USA Volume 1

myein (1999) see also p19
by Ann Hamilton
installations (detail), American Pavilion, 48th Venice Biennale, 1999
wood table, knotted cloth

Fist sized knots (one of the earliest
forms of record-keeping) were pulled
tightly against the table's surface
with their tails pulled through to fill
the space between the four legs and
slightly brush the ground beneath.

Contents

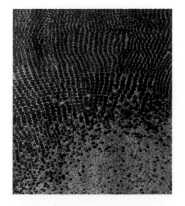

Susan Lordi Marker
Soulskin: Seeding the Prairie

Editor's Introduction

Ever since I fell in love with a textile artist I was smitten. The unfurling of that first wall hanging was my undoing. Promoting textile art has become a way of life and a labour of love.

I trained as a concert pianist and give several classical piano recitals a year. But while I was studying as a postgraduate in Budapest I developed a wrist injury which forced me to take a couple of years off – my guard was down, in slipped textiles. In a strange reversal of gender, I felt like a midwife for an international movement of textile artists. The one thing I heard over and over again was despair about the lack of recognition of the medium.

It didn't take me long to realise that textile art does not enjoy a level playing field in the world of art. In many countries it suffers from an astonishing prejudice in the eyes of the fine art world. I felt very strongly that I would like to do something, an act of protest, an act of calculated stealth on the fine art world...To paraphrase Matthew Collings in *What is Modern Art:* 'Picasso is Gauloises, Pollock is Marlboro, Warhol is the creation and marketing of a brand without any product, and textile artists are too busy working in the studio to stop for a smoke'.[1]

But work has become a dirty word in the art world. Nowadays the idea is the thing. Modern artists just have the ideas, that urinal idea, that *Merda d'Artista* idea [2] (respectively the number one and number two bright ideas from the art world). But they're too busy to become very engrossed in the mere manufacture of the object, beyond a quick grunt and a couple of press conferences. Another outmoded concept is beauty. Aesthetics, deeply felt communication from the artist to to the viewer? – all that stuff went out with the death of Matisse and Chagall. So where does that leave fibre art? Out in the cold.

It is interesting to compare the fate of photography with that of fibre art. Photography a century ago was too common a currency to have high value – everyone was familiar with matter-of-fact photographs, there was no art cachet to them. "The history of photography evolved independently and parallel to the history of painting. Fear of contact between the two was great, disputes sometimes harsh, a reconciliation seemed hopeless. Fortunately a dialog did eventually evolve and this is undoubtedly one of the most exciting chapters of the visual culture of our century. It was not just a matter of recognizing photography as art, but definitively eliminating the borders between photography and the creative arts. In time, photography succeeded in gaining public acceptance".[3]

Meanwhile, for now, galleries won't promote the medium of textiles, and as any good capitalist knows, if no one is selling or buying, you're cold turkey. If no one is buying, and no one is showing, and the media aren't picking it up, and the textile artists are demoralised, what are we all doing about it? Is it time to hang up those hanks of yarn and go and join those bad boys behind the bike sheds? Maybe. Who are textile artists: living saints, or wall-flowers with a death-wish? Last survivors of an ancient view of art as embodying integrity, sensitivity and skill; or confused, delusional nobodies experiencing a protracted death in no man's land?

But what is art anyway? Art involves transcendent skill and design, a persuasive aesthetic, and it often involves communication from the heart. The dictionary knows this; the history of art and culture knows this; the vast majority of art lovers know this. It is only a small minority who believe that the naked emperor of modern art is actually clothed. His time must surely soon be up.[4]

So we're allowed to be skilful and still be considered artists? YES! Art has always been skilful. Leonardo's notebooks ("My works are born of simple and pure experience, the true mistress...enabling men to strive toward what is possible, with discrimination") or

Bach's B-minor Mass ("If anyone works as hard as I have, they could achieve what I have achieved") or Liszt's *Etudes d'exécution transcendante* ("Homer, the Bible, Plato, Byron, Beethoven, Bach, Mozart...are all around me. I study them, meditate on them, devour them with fury; besides this I practise four to five hours of exercises: thirds, sixths, octaves, tremelos, repetition of notes, cadenzas, etc. Ah! provided I don't go mad you will find in me an artist!...") or Cézanne's studies of *Mont Sainte-Victoire* ("I work obstinately, I glimpse the Promised Land...") or Stravinsky's Oedipus Rex ("I am by nature prone to persist in overcoming difficulties") – great artists have always been passionately skilful! This is part and parcel of their art. They set themselves huge technical difficulties which they transcended. Their work has stood the test of time. It expresses universal human emotions or values. The richer their feeling, the more complex their layering of structural and technical procedures.[5]

Who knows how – in terms of journalism – this notion of a divorce between an artist's ideas and their skill has come about – it is a C-minus idea. It is of course true that artists such as Raphael would run a busy *atelier* with the assistance of apprentices. But this was only after acquiring mastery, and a reputation to match. (The idea that the likes of Raphael would condone unskilled art is absurd.) It is also true that a sculptor such as Louise Bourgeois may, being physically ill-equipped for the task of a gigantic sculpture, quite legitimately make a maquette and get others to make it for her. But this does not prove for one second that skill *per se* is inferior. This is an insidious misunderstanding which is to misrepresent the masterpieces of art, music and literature for centuries.[6]

What has happened is that the fine art world entered a sad cul-de-sac with Duchamp. Increasingly desparate, over-reliant on shock, a junkie's dependency on the quick fix of the latest technological buzz-word, morally bankrupt, technically deficient, an inability to relate positively to the roots of art history to a degree which would have any good therapist worried...The current art scene is all sex and no love; orphaned bastards lying around naked, bleating for attention. The public has bought into a kind of mass-delusion about the nature of art, a bit like a stock-market ramp or bubble. The latest name, the latest puff is hyped by a gallery with clout and good media connections; predictions of enhanced economic value of the work become self-fulfilling prophecies; economic values are seen as equal to real value. The artist is famous, therefore the art is good, therefore the price is high, and so it continues...

Gallery owners meanwhile, in England at least, appear to represent a last bastion of male chauvinism. We've had a drive for equal opportunities for the disabled, for women, for blacks – how about for textile artists? In Australia there is a very successful community of aboriginal women artists called Utopia. A small landscape painting on canvas by Emily Kngwarre auctions for around $23,000 USD, while a similar landscape on batik, which would have taken six times as long to make, sells for around $11,500 USD. Why? Because for gallery owners, canvas means art, silk means textiles. Textiles is women's work. It is merely a hobby. We don't sell textiles here Madam, good day.[7]

The gallery world may throw up two flawed arguments in defence of their exclusion of textile art: firstly that there is little market for this work. There are buyers and sellers for anything, if marketed and promoted effectively. There are many who have done very well out of buying work by certain textile artists early in their careers and seen their investments rise ten-fold. Out of those whose studios I have had the pleasure of visiting, it would seem a *very* safe bet that good work by the following will command substantially higher prices in ten years' time: installations by Yuko Takada Keller, now in Denmark; installations by Masakazu and Naomi Kobayashi in collaboration, and weavings by Chiyoko Tanaka, from Japan; silk hangings by Sally Greaves-Lord and installations by Yinka Shonibare in England; the early printed and painted work of Nicola Henley from Ireland; silk hangings by Utopia in Australia and mixed-media work by Marian Bijlenga in the Netherlands. (I am not rash enough to single out any artist from the States, but anyone who invested in Amazon.com at $100 may be ruing the day they neglected to buy some decent fibre art for their walls from any of the artists in this book – now *that* would have been a shrewd investment!)

The second argument put forward by the gallery world is that textiles are fragile and therefore a physically poor investment. Again this does not stand up to investigation. Like all art, textile art should be kept out of direct sunlight. The artist will leave simple, clear and competent instructions on maintenance, if necessary, for the gallery/owner. Woven tapestries, for example, many of which have already survived several centuries, may be lightly and carefully vacuumed. There is no mystique to this, nor cause for concern. After all, it is not as if the collection of paintings on canvas is trouble free. Think of the hugely expensive and sometimes damaging restoration of canvases that takes place all the time. Any investment carries with it risks and responsibilities and pleasures. But since many established artists such as Claes Oldenburg and Magdelena Abakanowicz use cloth, and since the value of their work rises, it can be seen that this explanation is merely another lame excuse for exclusion.

So not only are textile artists representing outlawed concepts of beauty, aesthetics and skill; as if that wasn't enough they are (mostly) the wrong gender in one of the few areas of western professional life where sexist discrimination and chauvinism reign totally unchallenged.

For the situation to improve, the first thing to go *must* be the word Craft. It hovers like an albatross in our wake. Craft, with its connotations of sandals, garage sales of cufflinks and pots, cost per square foot, hemp-dyeing workshops, sends out a confusing message to the public. Yes, textile artists have awe inspiring skills often with long traditions in the applied arts world, but let them be skills that dare not speak their name. The artistry is sometimes in concealing the difficulties. [8]

The presentation of art textiles, whether in print or on exhibition, has to regain an emphasis on art, on professionalism, with the ambition to move into a larger public sphere. I vote for 'art textiles' rather than 'textile art' as a name, as a kind of symbol. Exposure in the media, exposure in galleries, will need to be fought for and won with skill and determination. It is possible to retain artistic integrity and simultaneously to fight for recognition. As in music, photography and cinema, trends come and go. The public will one day become disenchanted with the current superficial scene (fast food, internet, techno-art) and start searching again for more meaning, warmth, lyricism, tactility, tradition...

My own personal contribution toward improving the public perception of textiles is my committment to publishing one volume a year in the series *Art Textiles of the World*. This is NOT intended to be an 'official top ten'. Instead, this is a personal selection of a variety of excellent artists from a country with hundreds of excellent artists. My criteria are as follows: I want to offer a wide variety of work across the spectrum of contemporary textile practise, be it tapestry, installations, printed and painted, mixed-media, weave, and so on. I try to include a fair balance of emerging, mid-career and established artists. (It might be tempting to stick to the safe big names, but where an artist already has a monograph of their work published, I feel that the public is already well served and it is somebody else's turn in the sun.) I have an unashamed bias toward work that is photogenic, since I consider that in the past a grave disservice has been done to the art textiles movement by the publication of so many 'how to do it' books full of out-of-focus, black and white photos.) Three-dimensional textile art is notoriously difficult to photograph effectively. On the whole this means a slight bias against installations (hard to get in focus) and against work which is predominantly white (disappears on the page) or which is monochrome (again this can look dull on paper over a whole chapter). On occasions and with great regret artists have had to be excluded due to the poor quality of photographic transparencies available. If the artist has sold much of their work overseas, or lost the address of the buyers etc, then alas there is little to be done. I hope that readers may find their conception of contemporary textile practice challenged and enlarged; that their appetite may be whetted to find out more about these artists' peers; that the personal slant of some of the artist's statements proves alluring to the general arts reader who in the past has often felt alienated by a preoccupation with matters technical. Finally, and perhaps most importantly, I dream that these books may serve as seeds for exhibitions of textile art – catalogues in search of an exhibition?!

I have a very simple ten year plan to dramatically improve the status of textile art. Here it is in a nutshell. I propose ten books in this series, one a year, each accompanying an exhibition of work by the ten artists. The exhibition to tour to ten cities around the world, with appropriate and sympathetic curators committing to this annual project. If you like this idea, you will need to wield your mouse!

Now to flesh it out a little: imagine a show in a city near you called *Art Textiles of the World: Japan* in the winter of 2003. Together with leading curator Keiko Kawashima of Gallery Gallery, Kyoto, Japan, I will be editing a book of the same title for publication in October 2003. If ten appropriate curators agreed to collaborate with Ms Kawashima (cherry-picking their favourite artists if necessary), not only would they have a fabulous exhibition in its own right, but also their galleries would be sure to enjoy a surge of visitors for the show, given the universal popularity of Japanese textiles (just ask MOMA). Interested galleries would almost certainly attract public funding and sponsorship. If the show toured to just one major city in each of the following countries: Great Britain, the Netherlands, Norway, Sweden, Finland, Japan, Australia, Canada and to two cities in the USA... If the show became a prized annual event in the cultural life of that city... A gradually expanding audience would come to see art textiles through fresh eyes. Media interest would surely follow. This will be the turning point of a vicious circle into a virtuous circle. Work of beauty, of aesthetic appeal, executed with integrity, speaking to the heart. Gaining new status in the eyes of the public through quality publications, educational events and deftly promoted international exhibitions. A new professionalism entering the textile world; an end to the ghetto mentality, no more defensiveness, increased self-confidence and awareness of what is happening from one country to another. Do you share our dream?

If so, the ball is in your court, dear reader. On Valentine's Day (February 14th) 2001 and annually thereafter, you are invited/incited to send an attractive mailing, either electronically or by snail mail, to the curators whom I will list on my web site (arttextiles.com in the 'feature' section) each January. If these curators hear from enough of you saying "I am asking you please to show an exhibition of Japanese art textiles in your Gallery", then surely they may act. Popular pressure can bring about real change in real life. 500 messages may not be enough. But 1,000, or 2,000, or 5,000 – that they surely could not ignore. To those who say "It's no use, Gallery prejudice will never change", I say "well, it is better to light a candle than to curse the darkness". Move your mouse in February, and please tell your colleagues. We've got a battle to win. The time has come.[9]

In the wonderful novel entitled *The Bear Comes Home,* the bear says "That's New York for you. If they think it's art they clap their hands, and if they think it might be real they turn pale and hope it goes away".[10] Textile art is for real and it's here to stay. Real art, with just as many ideas as fine art but better executed, finer art. I call it art textiles, or art for short.

Art Textiles of the world Art textiles of the world Art of the world Art. See?

This is not a book. It is an act of war.

Matthew Koumis
Editor

NOTES

1.   *What is Modern Art?* Matthew Collings, Weidenfeld und Nicholson.

2.   By Duchamp and Piero Manzoni, respectively.

3.   *20th Century Photography,* Marc Scheps, Taschen, 1996.

4.   "**Art** *n.* **1.** Skill, esp. human skill as opposed to nature; ability in skilful execution as an object in itself; cunning; imitative or imaginative skill applied to design, as in paintings, architecture etc; pertaining to use of such skill (art music; art needlework)". *Concise Oxford Dictionary* Professionals in the modern art world appear to have a surprising reluctance to distinguish between the two words A-R-T and S-T-U-N-T.

5.   Quote by Franz Liszt taken from *The Virtuoso Years,* Alan Walker, Faber & Faber,1989.
     Some interesting comments about the skill of Bach and Leonardo:
     "Not the least asset in Bach's musical setting of his texts was his contrapuntal ingenuity. This statement may seem surprising. We are accustomed to considering the consistent application of technical devices in music as an impediment to the free flow of imagination. But there is, as Goethe remarked, 'no form without content'. Bach was the last of the great line of composers who achieved beauty and depth not in spite of the contrapuntal devices he used but through them".
     The Bach Reader, Hans David and Arthur Mendel, W.W. Norton & Co, New York & London, 1972, pp34-35
     "To his contemporaries, art, *arte,* meant skill, much as we still use the concept in 'the art of war' or 'the art of love', while science, *scientia,* meant knowledge. Leonardo emphasised again and again in his writings that the art of painting had to rest on knowledge. Far from being a mere craft, painting should be classified with the so-called Liberal Arts, the disciplines based on knowledge".
     E.H. Gombrich, Preface to *Leonardo Da Vinci* (exhibition catalogue) South Bank Centre, London, 1989, p1.

6.   "She has always worked at more than one remove from the characteristic avant-garde movements of her lifetime: Surrealism, Abstract Expressionism, Pop, Minimal and Conceptual art Instead of a formally bound or conceptually coherent progression, her work has shown a progressive exploration of materials and techniques which has created for her an ever expanding field of practical options".
     Louise Bourgeois, Frances Morris, Tate Gallery Publishing 2000. Exactly the same could of course be said of a lot of textile artists.

7.   See *Art Textiles of the World: Australia,* ed. M. Koumis, Telos Art Publishing, 1999, p18.

8.   If only it were not obligatory for textile shows to have titles such as *Scrumptious Stitchery.* (*Painted Paint* by Picasso, a new exhibition of work executed with a half-inch sable brush. Workshops. Bring your own brush.)

9.   In fact our very first candle is being lit in October 2001, where the exhibition, *Art Textiles of the World: The Netherlands* (accompanied by the launch of our book of the same name edited by Dery Timmer) will take place at the Museum Rijswijk, in collaboration with Textiel Plus, and curated by Arjan Kwakernaak with Dery Timmer. (see museumryswyk.nl for further information).

10. By Rafi Zabor, published by Vintage.

The Art Textile:
A Conversation-in-Progress

"They are not using art to get a message across, rather, the getting across of the message is their art". Meyer Rubinstein.[1]

"Art is a very powerful cultural force in shaping our imaginations – so powerful because it speaks to both our conscious and unconscious...it is the dream life of our culture and it can be a subversive voice to help humanise our species". Jackie Brookner.[2]

Deborah Fisher
In my mind I'm dancing

Shifting paradigms

Since the Middle Ages, art practice in the West has been surrounded by theory and discourse. Currently, there is no clearly dominant art discourse, but there are conversations that should be of great interest to artists who work with textile media. In recent decades, as art and textile practice have become increasingly ideological and as artists are seen as content-providers, critical debate has focused on long-held modernist notions of production and reception of art: notably, that meaning and seeing are universal and that art is an esthetic event with no other purpose or association. Post-formalists argue that placing art in a realm apart from real life and viewing art in a disinterested state (Kant) is an unrealistic and irrelevant goal. As meaning is understood to be relational to culture and personal history, artists acknowledge the distinctive differences of each viewer, and invite a dialog with the work, precluding any fixed meaning. Art-as-praxis and community-oriented art has prompted non-traditional visual strategies, thus eroding media boundaries. The emerging discipline of visual culture is a response to the overlapping of art and popular culture and the intersection of disciplines such as psychology, anthropology, visual art, and physics.

Against this interdisciplinary and contextualized critical backdrop, artists, as never before, are presented with an abundance of choices. The ten artists included in this volume choose to manipulate cloth, build sculptural forms, assemble found objects, or stage interactive installations. They establish their esthetic positions within formalism, conceptualism, materiality, or hybrids thereof, and they express a diverse range of personal ideas that draw on politics, history, social theory, and semiotics. That these artists find their bearings, intellectually and emotionally, within textile history and practice, points to some contested areas of art criticism: the necessity of naming what artists do, and how to situate the art textile within the general art discourse.

Art as visual transformation

One of the most fundamental strategies of artmaking is transformation. These artists transform the familiar-objects, cloth, thread, physical space – and thereby alter our perceptions.

Susan Lordi Marker and Jason Pollen work with cloth as a blank slate. Marker shrinks, puckers, and burns cloth until it transmits a skin-like fragility and evokes the anthropological. Pollen applies brilliant dyes, paints, and fabric fragments to cloth; the result is shimmering and animated allusion to nature's transformations and movements. Both artists expose the malleability and receptivity of cloth to be stretched and colored into mosaic-like surfaces, presenting us with transcendent and beguiling fabric.

In the process of constructing cloth, thread by thread, Virginia Davis and Charlene Nemec-Kessel wed structure with image and color. Davis' minimalist ikats of painted warp and weft hover within the woven linen fabric as ghostly and poetic pure form. Nemec-Kessel's beautiful and complex fabrics update historic weaves with unconventional borders and modern symbolism.

Jane Sauer builds her sculptural forms incrementally, knot by knot. Color and structure are one, and threads accumulate into subtle surface texture. The low relief of thread/knot becomes a kind of mark-making, unfamiliar to other media.

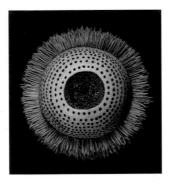

Kyoung Ae Cho
Pine Ball II

Uneasy objects

The objects, situations, and spaces created by these artists are not always easily categorized. The inclusion of sounds, smells, disintegrating natural materials, and human activities, render traditional art vocabulary inadequate.

Deborah Fisher, for example, combines and alters fragrant found objects, producing un-definable and fantastic assemblages, which she intends as an arena for close observation and consideration. And Linda Hutchins weaves barricade tape, which is not traditional tapestry or the authentic tape, but a satirical object that interchanges high and low.

Lengths of cloth are choreographed by Ann Hamilton; she swathes tables with it, suspends it in space, ties knots in it – cloth becomes a sensuous presence. Hamilton allows cloth to be folded and handled by attendants or destroyed by moths in small ecosystems that flourish and become spent within the space of a few weeks.

Jane Lackey and Kyoung Ae Cho employ found objects that are meant to be understood as what they are: transformation is by arrangement, giving the objects new identities. Lackey's unreadable slices of a dictionary, set into the wall, assemble into beautiful, rhythmic lines. Words lose their function and become repeated pattern. Cho collects nature's detritus – twigs, leaves, abandoned Christmas trees – and orders/arranges them into temporary installations or mysterious objects. She gives the viewer a second look at the overlooked. Both artists evoke new associations with nature and language, as we think we see/know it.

These ten artists speak to the visual and emotional strengths of textile and mine its characteristics for the sensual and the haptic. The fact that art involving textile processes can be exhibited and critiqued in different contexts is explained, in part, by multiple co-existing esthetic positions regarding fine art and craft. These diverse strands could account for the unclear status of both the textile and the hand-made object in contemporary art theory, and reveal biases about skill-based work.

Textile paradigms: many strands

The United States boasts a rich history of indigenous textiles, culturally integrated into daily life and spirituality. Always framed in an ethnographic context, these cultural products of Native Americans, Hispanics, African-Americans, have only relatively recently entered the fine art discourse. For example, multicultural estheticians have exposed the biases embedded in normalising language – such as "civilised" and "primitive." The use of non-fine-art materials and methods becomes a political act used to comment on cultural stereotypes and to produce redemptive images.

In the late 1960s, participants of the back-to-earth movement looked to traditional cultures and adopted craft as a lifestyle philosophy symbolic of community, self-sufficiency, and ecological responsibility. Textile as craft, functional and well-made, continues to be a working philosophy, reinforced by guilds nationwide. Such work was named "lesser" in the traditional art history; for the most part, the well-crafted object still occupies the fringes of art theory.

Since the 1940s, the art textile has hinged, philosophically, on European modernism. Art schools and universities gradually established textile departments, installing the foundation course approach of the Bauhaus. Textile practitioners could be artists or designers for industry. Textiles, however progressive in design, were often exhibited as yardage, to emphasize utility.

By the 1970s, the academic and art milieu of textiles had sparked unfettered experimentation. The large-scale, sculptural, visceral fiber works of the Art Fabric movement enjoyed unprecedented mainstream art acceptance as they easily fit with Greenbergian formalism, employed to theorize Abstract Expressionism. Artists, then, as now, may have based their work on unique personal history, textile metaphors, and political viewpoints, but the critical language concentrated on the visual and expressionistic. This brand of formalism still holds for many artists and critics.

For the last several decades, craft has been gaining currency as intellectual content. Marxist, feminist, and multiculturalist estheticians have politicized craft, exploiting the connotations of use-value, women's work, and the "other." Artists are speaking powerfully from the margins, and, in rejecting European modernism and notions of universality, reframe crafts. Clothing metaphors have been deployed widely, to investigate identity, loss, and memory, as well as to ironically flout modernist hierarchies. The critical discussion surrounding such work emphasizes the ideological and downplays traditional notions of object and making.

Jane Sauer
Tender Moments

Unsettled terrain

These co-existing textile paradigms have finally converged and account for the mercurial conversations in fiber and craft forums. Especially compelling are the debates that question: whether fibers do/should constitute a medium,[3] whether artists working in fiber should specialise less if they hope to enter the contemporary art discourse,[4] and whether the critical base for fibers has evolved enough to assert its merits within the contemporary art discourse.

In 1992, Janet Koplos contributed a timely and insightful essay to the discussion. In *Considering Crafts Criticism*, Koplos pointed out that "crafts has tended to be defined as a community rather than an aesthetic position". She argues that for four decades craft artists were misguided in trying to make painting and sculpture and that "what is useful and valuable and distinctive about crafts is often forgotten or disparaged". Some of the distinctive qualities of craft Koplos identifies are attention to surface and it subtleties, scale that is "keyed to the human body," and tangibility. Koplos suggests that "craft's best route to art is to capitalise on its strength, its own character, doing the things that other art mediums can't do".[5]

Locating meaning in materials and process: adding to the conversation

The artists here do speak to the formal and transformative strengths of textiles. Since the days of the Art Fabric, process (the act and philosophy of making) and materiality have been valued by artists as a way of generating visual ideas and being engaged with the work (resulting in expressiveness). In addition, the singularities of textile history and practice constitute a lexicon for personal and political ideas.

For example, in the knotted sculpture *Trujillo,* Jane Sauer wanted to express feelings about growth and change, resulting from a move to a new region. By knotting randomly, her methods represent, visually and intellectually, the struggle between order and chaos. One perceives that the action of non-ordered knotting provided Sauer with a physical connection to change. Her closed forms stand as metaphor for that which is interior, unexposed, inaccessible, secret.

Charlene Nemec-Kessel aims at expressing the absurdity of the human condition in her embroidered, double weave fabrics that reference historic textiles. In *Devour*, images of gossipmongers and florid, magnified borders of pattern enhance the narrative with traditional and personal symbols of femininity. Nemec-Kessel subverts western hierarchies that depreciate pattern by making the border equal to the central narrative, visually and conceptually. Her seemingly decorative fabrics remark on gender construction and her processes honor anonymous weavers; Nemec-Kessel identifies with weavings' working-class roots.

Repetitive tasks as relating to women's work are of importance to many of the artists here; weaving and knotting are not used ironically, but recognized as part of a human continuum and symbolic of gender roles. Susan Lordi Marker sees cloth as having the same elemental importance as skin and earth. In *Manifesto*, repeated manipulation and layering of opaque and sheer fabrics results in levels of pictorial space that appear to be simultaneously fading away and materializing. Marker's themes involve fragility and the ephemeral – cloth, clothing, and that which is preserved and passed down, stands as the evidence of a human life.

In *Terra Luminosa*, Jason Pollen uses pattern and repetition to make visible the natural disintegration of leaves and stones in a "perpetual state of transformation," which he relates to human experience, as well. Clearly, the placing of silk cloth fragments is done by hand, providing an attentive, human, even loving, connection to this intimate view of nature. The fluidity of cloth, the way it absorbs dye into its structure and yields to gravity, lends itself to a visual expression of the constant, rhythmic cycles of nature.

Kyoung Ae Cho also investigates the rhythms and patterns of nature. While mindfully giving found objects new life, Cho honors the cultural influences of craftsmanship and respect of materials inherited from her grandmother. During the "ceremonial" act of collecting natural objects, the artist engages in "visual and sensual conversations" with nature. While observing falling leaves, which gather as a blanket to protect the earth, Cho discovers metaphors shared with the quilt form (*Chaos II*).

For Linda Hutchins making art is, alternatively, a spiritual and intellectual activity. Having become disenchanted with image-making, Hutchins investigates structure and objects as carriers of meaning. Her suite of tapestries depicting domestic scenes as elemental shapes (*Three Chairs Facing Right*), are small enough to magnify the presence of slits and delineations of weft boundaries. The crowded pictorial space expresses confinement and propriety, themes that find other incarnations in Hutchins' work. In *Bread Cage*, wire harshly binds crumbling bread to produce a poignant image of attempted entrapment.

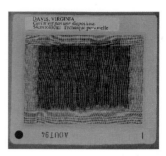

Virginia Davis
This is not a Slide

Jane Lackey
Possibilities and Reversals

Virginia Davis displays an appreciation for traditional textiles – stunning Indian ikats and sacred cloths she has seen in her travels inform her work visually and intellectually (*Scroll*). Davis enjoys the processes of ikat, painted weft, and weaving, finding the combination of planning and serendipity satisfying. But she also reframes her textiles as comments on the materials and business of art (*This is not a Slide*). She weaves linen canvas with painted threads; these deconstructed paintings subvert traditional art definitions by blurring the line between painting and craft. Davis explains that "from a 1990s perspective, my work examines and reinterprets minimalism in the context of the symbolic significance of textile imagery".

The work of these artists reminds us that there are many valid processes: an idea may precede its form, or an idea may result from an intellectual conversation with materials.

The Academy considers new paradigms

In recent art discourse, idea-driven art is privileged, and so, it is not necessary to define work by medium. In a body of work about identity, an artist might film a video, take photographs, sew clothing, make a painting, and lobby Congress. The open-ended definitions of art, and the focus on concept and message, have prompted a vigorous discussion about the relevance of the traditional foundation courses and media-based curricula in our art schools.[6] If all meaning is relative, if emerging technologies and increasing globalization have prompted new forms and meanings in art, then approaching work by medium alone may be limiting the expression of ideas and, as an educational stance, underemphasizes the development of conceptual skills.

In fact, many fiber departments have disappeared from universities over the last decade, or have removed looms and merged with sculpture and mixed-media departments. This doesn't necessarily deny the history or practice of textiles, but it does emphasize the theoretical and a way of working that is concept-oriented, rather than medium-oriented. These new approaches to art education seek to turn out more socially responsible artists who are able to engage and expand the art audience.

New contexts for objects and the material

In recent decades, the discrete art object has come to represent, fairly or not, the commerce of art or putting art on a pedestal, in a frame, separated from life. By asserting idea, metaphor, and making, these artists show us that making objects is still worthy of discussion.

For Deborah Fisher, small-scale objects can stimulate intellectual and emotional associations and invite an intimate dialog with the viewer. Fisher constructs vaguely recognizable, surreal tools, which the viewer can imagine holding and using (*Tools for if you are afraid of the dark*). Associations with touching and use suggest a more than passive kind of looking that accounts for the differences of the viewer – "that one individual".

Jason Pollen
Dharma Light

Jane Lackey does not follow one method or medium. Rather, her art investigates language, technology, history, and science, in work that does not always draw, obviously, from the textile tradition. In *possibilities and reversals*, for example, her materials are plexiglass and acrylic on masonite. Isolated, magnified images of human chromosomes are framed and arranged to suggest an alphabet or writing – the viewer can touch and turn the images. In much of the artist's work, scale makes the unseen visible – the microscopic can be read as landscape, language, or beautiful marks. Such work investigates knowing and experience – it does not ask be to labelled fiber, although the physical presence of these objects/situations and the references to the body, are in line with a textile ethos of making or materialization.

Ann Hamilton has a background in textile design and clearly appreciates the associative value of cloth. Her extremely diverse body of work, both installations and objects, are not easily categorized – but textile sensibilities are apparent. Hamilton investigates the ways we perceive, intellectually and haptically, wanting to "make language more material and draw out the language in material".[7] Repetition is a recurring motif of textile artists – for Hamilton, this could be the constant billowing of cloth, a cascading rain of pigment, or human activity. In *mattering*, for example, an attendant methodically pulls a continuous length of blue typewriter ribbon from an inkpot on the floor and winds it around his hand. The viewer watches this process and sees the evidence in his stained hands – the seemingly mundane, individual task as ritual. Hamilton's environments are conceived with reference to the architectural space and the knowledge that the viewer enters and inhabits the spaces with these objects and actions. Rooms become highly charged – smells and whispering recorded voices fill the rooms, making the unseen palpable. Hamilton's work is widely respected – she was chosen to represent the United States at the 48th Venice Biennale (*myein*). Hamilton engages her audience intellectually, while acknowledging that one of the ways we "know" is by touch.

Which discourse? Which audience?

The modernist criteria applied to painting and sculpture may not have always been appropriate for contemporary art based in textile processes. A history rich in guilds, collaboration, female producers, and function, counters some of the tenets of modernism: originality, genius (art cannot be taught), and art-for-art's-sake. By exploiting the singular meanings of textile forms, structures, and processes, these artists are sometimes placed outside the general art discourse. Yet much of the new work in the textiles field deserves attention and covers new conceptual ground. Computer technology was prefigured by the jacquard loom and, at the start of a new century, invites new relationships between art and technology. *The Virtual Nomad: Textiles and Technology* was a recent exhibition at the Linda Hall Library of Science, Engineering, and Technology in Kansas City, Missouri, that brought together art, science and mathematics with interactive displays and information banks. The viewer was an active participant in manipulating virtual textiles and transmitting touch onto computer screens. In her commentary about the exhibition, co-curator Catherine Amidon notes that the new interface of textiles with technology and science, suggests new contexts for entrenched concepts such as pictorial space, the creative act, and pattern/repetition, which is being re-examined in terms of biological events.[8]

Semiotics has put the spotlight on notions of truth, and artists are considering new paradigms for communication that reconnect the verbal with the emotional. Artists are positioning their work within new modes of visual, emotional, and intellectual communication. Susan Lordi Marker etches and prints her family stories into her fabric, believing that oral traditions survive because they have continued relevance. It is not important that the viewer decipher the words, she explains, but that that "they connote communication beyond the written word". Increased interest in spectatorship and the mandate to establish art as a dialog between individuals reframes traditional notions of object and making.[9] The artists represented here may not have enough in common in terms of medium and method to be named together. But, if there is a common theme, it might be a shared understanding with their audience. These artists direct their work toward anyone who has a memory of cloth, an emotional connection to objects, and to those who can make room for a dreamlife. The art textile can be transgressive, subversive, and challenging, or empathetic, connective, seductive. Each viewer has a cultural, personal, and physical uniqueness that is a valued contribution to the meaning of the work. Charlene Nemec-Kessel weaves narratives that transform as she repeats them to herself during long hours at the loom. Changes that occur in the telling of a tale, Nemec-Kessel explains, are significant "and because the story teller ultimately responds to what listeners want to hear the changes also reveal something about the listeners".

It seems that fine art theory, always in flux, may still need to make space to recontextualize skill-based work. Quality, a concept under fire as representing elitist Euro-centric connoisseurship, could take on new meaning, just as the decorative can be ideological. As these artists continue to investigate, within new contexts, the meaning of making, the talismanic, and the sensory, the art textile is still a conversation-in-progress.

Ilze Aviks

Artist and writer

Fort Lewis College, Durango, Colorado

NOTES

1. Meyer Raphael Rubinstein, 'Hachivi Edgar Heap of Birds', *Flash Art*, Nov–Dec 1990, p155.
2. Jackie Brookner, 'Feminism and Students of the 80s and 90s: The Lady and the Raging Bitch; Or, How Feminism Got a Bad Name', *Art Journal*, Summer 1991, p12.
3. Catherine S. Amidon, 'Is there still a place for fiber art?' *FIBERARTS*, Nov/Dec 1997, pp42–47.
4. William Easton, 'Shifting Perceptions', *FIBERARTS*, Summer 1995, pp44–49.
5. Janet Koplos, 'Considering Crafts Criticism', *Haystack Institute Monograph Series* 1992, pp3–10.
6. Timothy Allen Jackson, 'Ontological Shifts in Studio Art Education: Emergent Pedagogical Models', *Art Journal*, Spring 1999, pp68–73.
7. Ann Hamilton quoted from a television interview with Charlie Rose, October 4, 1999. PBS Broadcast Transcript #2522.
8. Catherine Amidon, 'Using Textiles To Navigate Our Way To the Next Century', *FIBERARTS*, Sept/Oct 1999, pp38–43.
9. Carol Becker, 'The Education of Young Artists and the Issue of Audience', *Between Borders Pedagogy and the Politics of Cultural Studies*, New York: Routledge, 1994, pp101–112.

Linda Hutchins
Three Ways

Artists

Ann Hamilton

How do we understand what we know but can't name? We are born into material as we are into language; they are of each other, yet we inherit a perception of them as separate. Allowing language to be tactile and knowledge to be felt is the process of my work.

a round (1993)
installation at Power Plant, Toronto, Canada
sawdust stuffed wrestling dummies, canvas floor, column-mounted
mechanized punching bags, seated figure, circular hand knitting

My world is full of questions: How is? How do? How can? What is?

How is language material? How is art a form of remembering or reminding? For me, the act of writing is one of remembrance and of embodiment. Ones' hand moves at the pace of the body to both ingest and expel the word. Like speaking and writing, sewings' trajectory is exterior. The line of writing, like thread, is absorbed at the same time that it is laid out through the physical act of making. In 'slaughter' Susan Stewart's poem of the same name is stitched to the glove as a kind of membrane or net – by being written out in a continuously cursive line the words lose their singularity and dissolve into an illegible web. The words in these pieces are not mine, but in a way they have become part of me through the stitching of them.

So when I ask how is unmaking a form of making? in a sense the text is erased as it is written, the spaces between the letters wrap the hand and become more visible than the letters themselves. What is the relationship between word and experience? Often in my work, words are out of reach, or on the perimeter.

How do we understand what we know but can't name? We are born into material as we are into language; they are of each other yet we inherit a perception of them as separate. It is difficult for words to contain our somatic perceptions, our senses of touch and smell, yet we are impatient with experiences whose forms aren't readily nameable.

Allowing language to be tactile and knowledge to be felt is the process of my work.

slaughter (1997)
silk organza glove
(one of an edition of 12)
embroidered

myein (1999) (detail – see also frontispiece)
installations, American Pavilion, 48th Venice Biennale, 1999
fuchsia powder, sound, braille text of poetry by Charles Reznikoff
(*Testimony* – The United States, 1885-1915, recitative volumes I & II)

At the perimeter of the four galleries, the fuchsia powder sifted slowly, turbulently, formless and incessant in its movement. This slowly seeping, leaking, continual descent of toxic colored powder eluded any easy or familiar association. Apart from this dusting and accumulation of powder, the interior rooms seemed empty...but with the removal of existing ceilings, sunlight flooded the interior. The recording of a whispering voice circled round to haunt and fill the space with sound.

By insinuating inclusion or exclusion, the whispering voice subverted the public character of the space and, like the powder, was both pervasively present yet out of reach. For this recording, excerpts from Abraham Lincoln's second Inaugural Address were spoken in phonetic code where each letter is spelled out as a name or thing: Alpha for A, Indigo for I, Bravo for B, and so on. The text could be deciphered only by notating in writing each coded letter. Originally delivered near the close of the American Civil War, Lincoln's address extended a healing hand toward that primary schism in American democracy the institution of slavery. In my installation in Venice, this coded speech became as opaque and difficult to know as a reading of the white plaster dots which lined the interior walls with the replication of an enlarged Braille text. While the original uses of Braille and the phonetic alphabet are both military in origin, here they account for a historical record of racial and property violence. Although impossible to read as text, the individual constellations of plaster dots were marked over six months of the exhibition as the continual cascade of descending fuchsia powder collected to stain and ring their presence. If the act of writing replaces absent sound, then here both speech and text are concealed by codes of sound and touch and rendered opaque. They evoke an unnameable legacy of grief in my account of those schisms of democratic space which are part of The United States' short history.

The dominant movements of *myein* are the downward pull of time and gravity and the incessant horizontality of landscape and writing. *Myein* is an Ancient Greek verb meaning to close the eyes or mouth. Across time, myein has to come to stand for that which has not been, or cannot be, explained. This installation attempts to create a space that is simultaneously empty and full.

mattering (1998) below and cover
undulating silk, peacocks, recorded voices, typewriter ribbon
1st installed at Musée d'Art Contemporain, Lyon, France
subsequently installed at Musée d'Art Contemporain de Montréal, Canada

This project explores the relationship between word-centred and haptically experienced perception.

A suspended horizon of orange silk bisected the volume of space. Attached at one end to a mechanical drive, the cloth slowly raised to fill with air and then fell to fill the space with undulating, wave-like movement. On the underside of this canopy, five shimmering blue and green male peacocks strutted freely or sat on one of six wall-mounted perches. Mixed with the sounds of peacocks (screeching at times) and the hushed billowing of air filling the cloth, the faint, recorded sound of a vocal exercise – where the voice of the student mimicked the voice of his teacher – could also be heard floating downward from the ceiling of the gallery. The only other element within the room was a vertical wooden pole attached to the floor and rising to the ceiling through a hole in the cloth. There, perched above the orange silk, a sitting attendant pulled a continuous line of indigo blue typewriter ribbon through the lip of a porcelain ink pot covering a small hole to the floor below. The ribbon was woven round the fingers of the attendant to stain, bind and encircle his hand. When the hand was completely covered, he removed the blue ball of ribbon and passed it down through the orange membrane to the floor. As this gesture was repeated, a mound of typewriter ribbon accumulated at the base of the pole.

Born   1956, Lima, Ohio

Education and Awards

1979   BFA, Textile Design, University of Kansas

1985   MFA, Sculpture, Yale School of Art, New Haven, Connecticut

1989   Guggenheim Memorial Fellowship

1993   MacArthur Fellowship

1993   NEA Visual Arts Fellowship

Selected Solo Exhibitions

1999   *welle,* Carnegie International, Carnegie Museum of Art, Pittsburgh

1999   *myein,* The United States Pavilion, 48th Venice Biennale, Italy

1999   *whitecloth,* The Aldrich Museum of Contemporary Art, Ridgefield, Connecticut

1998   *mantle,* Miami Art Museum, Florida

1997   *kaph,* Contemporary Arts Museum, Houston, Texas

1997   *bounden and mattering,* with *Ann Hamilton, Present-Past 1984-97,*
           Musée d'Art Contemporain, Lyon, France

1996   *The Body and the Object, Ann Hamilton 1984-96,* Wexner Center for the Arts, Columbus, Ohio

1996   (tour to Wood Street Galleries and Carnegie Museum of Art, Pittsburgh, Pennsylvania;
           Krannert Art Museum, Champaign, Illinois; Miami Art Museum, Florida;
           and Musée d'Art Contemporain de Montréal, Canada)

1996   *filament,* Sean Kelly, New York

1996   *reserve,* Stedelijk van Abbe Museum, Eindhoven, The Netherlands

1995   *lumen,* Institute of Contemporary Art, Philadelphia

1994   *seam,* Project 48, The Museum of Modern Art, New York

1994   *mneme,* Tate Gallery, Liverpool

Selected Commissions

1998   *Appetite,* performance collaboration with Meg Stuart & Damaged Goods,
           European and US tour 1998-99

1994-   Allegheny Riverfront Park, The Pittsburgh Cultural Trust
           (in collaboration with Michael Van Valkenburgh, Michael Mercil, Matthew Urbansky)

1990-95   San Francisco Public Library Commission, The Arts Commission of San Francisco
           (in collaboration with architects James Freed, Kathy Simon and artist Ann Chamberlain)

1989-90   Mess Hall, Headlands Center for the Arts, Sausalito, California

Work in Public Collections

           The Museum of Modern Art, New York

           Stedelijk van Abbe Museum, Eindhoven

           Musée d'Art Contemporain de Montréal, Canada

           Musée d'Art Contemporain, Lyon, France

           The Walker Art Center, Minneapolis

Ann Hamilton is represented by Sean Kelly Gallery, New York

arc*hive* (1999)
Installation view of hive, blot, diaries

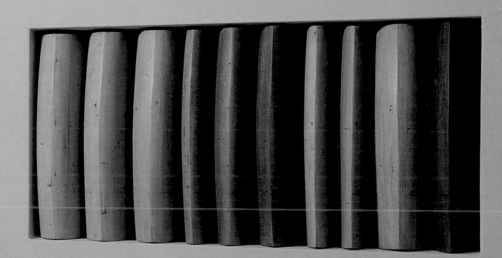

"The present epoch will perhaps be above all the epoch of space. We are in the epoch of simultaneity: we are in the epoch of juxtaposition, the epoch of near and far, of side by side, of the dispersed." We are at a moment, I believe, when our experience of the world is less that of a long life developing through time than that of a network that connects points and intersects with its own skein. 'Of Other Spaces,' Michel Foucault [1]

For many years my work has been informed by practices within the field of fiber, a prolific site of interdisciplinary activity. Textile mediums offer a specific sphere of investigation which through their multiplicity have contributed to opening more flexible definitions of art practice. The history of textiles combines a legacy of cultural encoding, labor intensive processes, contextual relationships, and currently evolving linkage to digital media and technology. This range offers many conceptual frameworks for new configurations of materials, ideas, perceptual phenomena and cultural experience. Although I might be classified more readily as a painter now, my work is inextricably involved with process. Habits of working developed through a methodology of handling and exploring materials and their modes of construction have provided a context for hybridity. Perhaps the work is more fully understood within a cross-sectional relationship of disciplines which are centred around the subject of the body.

There is an interesting correspondence between acquired memory and memory that is genetically encoded within the cells of our bodies. Both types of memory are pivotal to identity. Yet the distinction between the fixed and the mutable blurs as technology facilitates revolutionary levels of revision and change. We have come to know ourselves differently in this time when scientific research is rapidly probing the once invisible space of the body, presenting possibilities which upset our notions of culture, nature, identity, and uniqueness. My work engages aspects of our beings which are inaccessible yet are fully sensed and known in other measurable ways. It involves the psychological dispositions of self as seen within the liquid culture of the laboratory.

Abstraction gives us the ability to empty out references, to collapse familiarity, to perceive phenomena within a new-found configuration of form. My interest in abstraction stems from the desire to articulate an invisible dimension. Tactile qualities of materials, coded marks and systems of numbers and letters find their place as the tools of measurement. Medical science provides a model of researchers who observe and code the body's complex interior information though succinct methods of notation. In an analogous way, I condense complexities into simple and spacious form containing traces of tangible physical movements along the surfaces. Within this space, issues in textiles, painting and science form a relationship. An interest in cloth naturally involves the study of the codes of pattern. Human DNA is one of the largest archives of such. The chemical structure of everyone's DNA is the same and is mapped through ordering the letters which stand for the nitrogenous base pairs of adenine (A), thymine (T), cytosine (C), and guanine (G). The only difference between individuals is the ordering of these four bases. There are so many millions of base pairs in each person's DNA that we each have a unique sequence.

In this series, the shapes of the works have been formed to curve away from the wall and encapsulate space while their outer edges reflect two notions...half body curve and half straight edge of coded notation.

blot 3 (1999)
acrylic, ink, cork, birch
114 x 113 x 10cm (45 x 44.5 x 4")

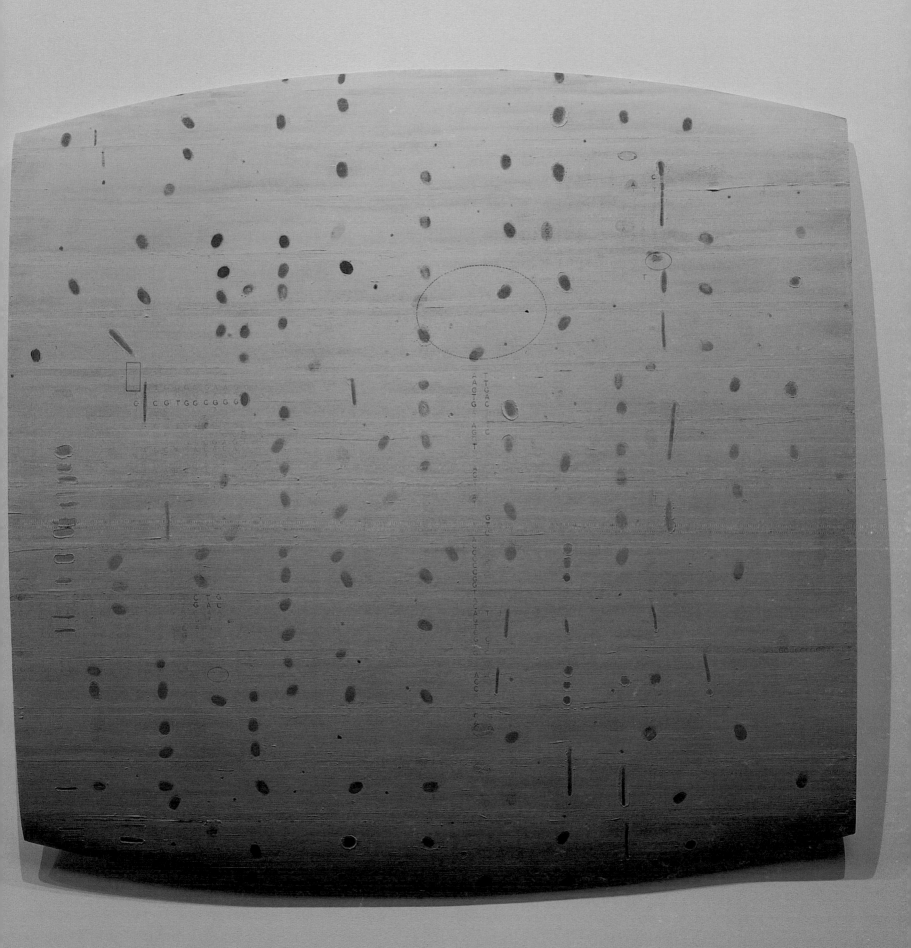

23 reversible images which the viewer can view and turn. Each pair of images examines one of the 23 pairs of chromosomes. We usually see human chromosomes laid out in a particular format (more grid-like). It was my intention to separate each pair as a distinct element, to see the sequence as a linear alphabet for a written language or a calligraphic mark.

possibilities and reversals (1996)
double-sided iris prints in plexiglass and aluminium frames; acrylic on masonite
12.5 x 252 x 15cm (5 x 99 x 6")

marker 6 (1996)
acrylic, cork, masonite
196 x 86 x 2.5cm (77 x 34 x 1")

Composed from equal-sized sections, the columns (an ongoing series) suggest an endless and continuous feed of genetic mapping and combine references with technology, time and history.

column 2 (1997)
acrylic, cork, ink, pastel, masonite
183 x 30.5 x 2.5cm (72 x 12 x 1")

To fully map each person's DNA would be an enormously time-consuming project and borders on the absurd fantasies of making maps identical in size to the territory being mapped. Fortunately there are repeating sequences in DNA so forensic scientists have been able to develop shorter methods of matching identities. The complex process of mapping identities is reduced to recognition of patterns, blots, smears, columns and strings of letters. The guttural physicality of the names given to describe these scientific processes (smears, blots, fingerprinting) serve as cues to my gestural marks of paint – fingerprinting/ finger-painting. Interior code becomes translated through exterior signifier. The words (blot, smear, marker) express a double meaning when applied to self and identity. This intersection of disciplines brings us to a synthesis of bodily imprints, fluid stains of color, stripes, dots, dashes, accidents, anomalies, chance operations.

To insert the words and ideas of science into the process of making is to give new thought to the significance of materials, craft, theory, and science which challenge and rearrange how memory is embedded within form. The equation of space with information and knowledge suggests the form and volume of a book and the spatial orientation of language. A recent installation entitled 'archive' brings together a group of works presented within the meaning of the title which implies a collection or repository of information, a strategy of organization or a place of order and protocol. By further breaking the word into two parts — arc and hive — the title asserts a visual predominance of curving forms (arc), paired with the stacked, layered or buried containment implied by the second part of the word (hive). Some of the works within this installation are partially buried in a negative recess in the surface of the wall or there is hidden space within the work itself. Referring to information that is progressively more invisible, the formation of the space entombs the form, enclosing the information. Space becomes body and book.

The titles of the works within the 'archive' installation are *smear (1)*, *smear (2)*, *blot*, *webster's line*, *hive*, *diaries* and *index and function* as titles have in previous works (*traits*, *markers*, *columns*, *tablets*). Each relates to a complex yet highly organized system of information and provides a lens for framing the reduced forms and seemingly indeterminate, gestural marks found within their surfaces. In the most recent work *DNA*, the dictionary, or a colony of bees, provide the matrix for contemplating codes of information both visible and invisible and observing deviations that penetrate the filter of order.

1. Michel Foucault, 'Des Espaces Autres,' *Architecture-Mouvement-Continuité*, October, 1984 (source: Diacritics, Spring 1986, Published by John Hopkins University Press).

webster's line (1999) (section)
found dictionaries, polyurethane
24 x 71 x 4cm (9½ x 28 x 1½")

Pages have been cut into sections, turned, and positioned tightly side by side so that they extend 15 feet across the gallery wall and are built into the surface of the wall. The words, the components of language, are sliced so that they are indistinguishable, appearing only as random patterns of ink on the edges of severed pages. Language being both exposed and hidden is scanned from the perspective of the slice.

Born   1948, Chattanooga, Tennessee

Education and Awards

1974   B FA, California College of Arts and Crafts, Oakland, California
1979   M FA, Cranbrook Academy of Art, Bloomfield Hills, Michigan
1984, 88   National Endowment for the Arts, Individual Artists Fellowship Grant
1989   United States/France Visual Artist Residency, La Napoule Art Foundation, La Napoule, France
1995   Margaret Hall Silva Foundation Grant for *in code* exhibition
1997   Illinois Arts Council, Individual Artist Grant

Selected Exhibitions

2000   *Paradise Now,* EXIT ART, New York
2000   *Remnants of Memory,* Asheville Art Museum, Asheville, North Carolina
2000   *Jane Lackey/Joan Livingstone,* Roy Boyd Gallery, Chicago, Illinois (two persons)
1999   *archive,* Cranbrook Art Museum, Bloomfield Hills, Michigan (solo)
1998   *Trans-,* Network Gallery, Pontiac, Michigan and N C Gallery, Pusan, South Korea
1998   *Jane Lackey,* Sybaris Gallery, Royal Oak, Michigan (solo)
1997   *Off the Map,* Paint Creek Center for the Arts, Rochester, Michigan
1997   *tabulations,* Roy Boyd Gallery, Chicago, Illinois (solo)
1996   *in code,* Grand Arts, Kansas City, Missouri (solo)
1994   *Jane Lackey: Recent Works,* I Space, Chicago, Illinois (solo)
1993   *Jane Lackey – A Decade of Work,* Textile Art Center, Chicago, Illinois (solo)
1993   *Pushing the Boundaries,* Evanston Art Center, Evanston, Illinois
1992   *Domestic Ontogeny,* Oliver Art Center, California College of Arts and Crafts, Oakland, California
1991   *Perspectives from the Pacific Rim,* Bellevue Art Museum, Bellevue, Washington
1989   *14th Biennale Internationale de la Tapisserie,* Musée Cantonal des Beaux-Arts,
              Palais de Rumine, Lausanne, Switzerland

Publications

1999   "*archive,* an installation of new work by Jane Lackey", Irene Hofmann (essay for Gallery publication)
1999   Cranbrook Art Museum, Bloomfield Hills, Michigan (Gallery catalogue)
1997   "Lost in a Sea of Shapes", Fred Camper, *Chicago Reader* (19.9.97)
1996   "in code", Laurie Palmer, Grand Arts, Kansas City, Missouri (essay for Gallery publication)

Professional

1997-   Artist-in-Residence, Head of the Department of Fiber, Cranbrook Academy of Art, Michigan

Work in Public Collections

              Detroit Institute of the Arts, Detroit, Michigan
              James A. Michener Collection, Kent State University, Kent, Ohio
              Arthur Andersen and Company, Chicago, Illinois

Jason Pollen

We are like alchemists, seeking to refine and transform what we see into precious substances with magical properties.

Terra Luminosa (1991)
silk, fiber reactive dyes, vat dye discharge
painted, printed, fused
67.5 x 105cm (27 x 42")

Manipulated surfaces are like mirrors which can provide insights into this present moment. Whether or not we are paying attention to what is reflected back to us is the issue. So painting or printing a mark on cloth, erasing a mark, dyeing a piece of cloth and stitching into it, those activities present us with opportunities to be here with our minds and bodies, and to explore the relationships of the inside to the outside, the tangible and the illusory. We are like alchemists mining and refining crude ore, seeking to transform it into precious substances with magical properties. We develop unique tools to mine our surfaces, excavating layer beneath layer, like diligent prospectors, fairly certain that what still lies hidden will be revealed in time. Even though in the vastness of this unfathomable universe we are no more than cosmic dust, that dust contains all the secrets of the ages past, present, and future, and clues to the great riddles show up in our creative experiments, in the laboratory which is the artist's studio. I believe it is my job to investigate the clues to the mysteries of the obscured cosmos and coax out meaning in a coherent visual language. Ripples on sea and sand sing the song of the powerful but invisible winds that form them. Wrinkles on foreheads, creases on shoes, tell our complex stories; rings under our eyes and around Saturn remind us of our limitations, remind us of corporal and cosmic clocks ticking, telling us we have little time to do what we must do, that we have no time to waste, that we must use time wisely, and in service to others.

To dig deeply takes time, takes will, takes patience, takes stamina. Silk screens, dyes, colored pencils and computer programs are tools which help me learn to look for essences among the endless phenomena which signal us from our inner and outer worlds. We learn to listen to and to look at the subtler stuff which seeks to expand our awareness. Illusions and truths ascend and descend to the surface of our minds and to the silk's surface. So I scratch and scour, dive, delve and differentiate, prod, pierce and peel, extract and examine. And I am eager to share my findings with others, to give away what I discover to those who share this passion. The traces we leave will eventually fade, like footsteps in the sand, but brave, new insights will come, daring us to decipher and make sense of the confusion, and to depict the magic of the surfaces inside surfaces within surfaces.

The activity of building images out of silk and dye and thread reconnects me with the little boy who spent his childhood summers skimming stones off the crests of waves, and constructing elaborate castles of sand and shells, tuning into the powerful silent gray sky, beyond thoughts, beyond the thunderous rhythmical crashing noise of the ocean slamming the shore. The beach taught me lessons on the ephemeral nature of all composite things, on the arising, residing and subsiding of all phenomena. No sooner were the castles built than the sea erased every vestige of them. Why make another one just to see it topple and disintegrate? How could I not?

Now I use color and cloth and dye, lines and shapes, and compose and arrange forms, sometimes orderly, sometimes not so orderly. I am compelled to enter and re-enter the zone where creation is always longing to add to the innumerable material manifestations so distinctly a part of the drama, the comedy and tragedy being played out on this planet.

Even though in the vastness of this unfathomable universe we are no more than cosmic dust, this dust contains all the secrets of the ages past, present, and future. Clues to the great riddles show up in our creative experiments, in the laboratory which is the artist's studio.

revelation (1993)
silk, fiber reactive dyes, vat dye discharge
painted, printed, fused
140 x 100cm (56 x 40")

Most recently I have been experiencing the cloth and the water and the dye, the drying and the steaming, as if they were meteorological phenomena; so I now feel like a weather-man or rather a maker of weather on fabric. One day late last summer I was swimming in the ocean at the south New Jersey shore. Very few people were in the water because it was teeming with jellyfish, coming to dry up and die under the August sun. This reminded me of the plight of lemmings, and of so many living beings microscopic and visible, whose inner clocks tell them it's time for the big change. Swimming with the jellyfish, looking up at threatening thunder heads, I perceived similarities in them. There is a large mass at the top, full with water, and then either streams of rain falling in broken lines to meet the sea and the land, or in the case of the jellyfish, tentacles reaching down to attract food and to deal harshly with potential prey. My recent work resembles a hybrid of both clouds and jellyfish. This was not intentional; the images just showed up. Artists are either premeditators, those who think ahead before they make what they make, and know pretty much what a piece will look like and what it's about; or those who just go for a swim and discover connections between this and with that, and feel compelled to make work embodying aspects of those experiences. I clearly fall into the second category. I have been doodling since early childhood, almost uncontrollably. I am most often surprised, even astonished, by the finished pieces. I feel that I can take no blame or credit for them. It is as though I (the persona part at least) disappear, go for a long mental walk, and when I come back a new work is there. This experience will be familiar to many of you. The process has repeated itself over a lifetime, and it is as much a mystery to me now as it ever was. But the child in me insists it is quite sane and natural; the judgmental grown-up in me is prone to suspect a neurotic aspect to the habitual pattern in it. There is of course no turning back, so it is likely that the clouds and jellyfish will stay around for a while, and quite likely be succeeded by a new cast of unfamiliar and unexpected metaphorical visitors.

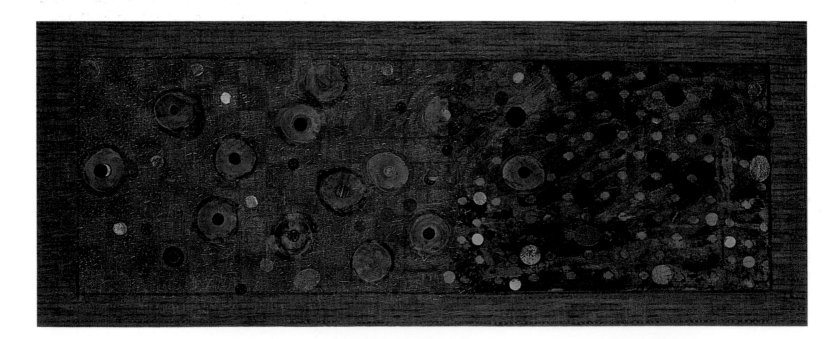

Dance the Dance (1997)
silk, fiber reactive dyes, vat dye discharge
painted, printed, fused
67.5 x 240cm (27 x 96")

I am compelled to enter and re-enter the zone where creation longs to contribute to the comedy, tragedy and drama being played out on this planet.

I am deeply interested in the chemical and physical properties of dye and fiber, as well as the substances which can discharge dye and disintegrate fiber. Painting was my second love in college; dance was my first love. Eventually painting moved to first place. But paint sits on the surface, ignoring any possible deep relationship with the cotton or linen which it covers. When I moved to Europe and then India in the sixties and seventies I became entranced with luminous, lustrous silks which seduced me with their radiant colors and provocative patterns. Once I learnt how to provoke and master the mating of dye and fiber molecules, painting and printing took a quite unanticipated turn. The rest, as they say, is history. I am now dedicated to the silkworm and to the substances which can color its filaments. It is with great joy that I, not unlike the silkworm, feel as naturally inclined to spin out piece after piece, hoping that once in a while visual poetry with communicative power may manifest as a by-product.

Rain falls from the sky to the sea, merging with it. Marine life, animate and inanimate, washes up onto the shore. Everything everywhere ebbs and flows.

left:
Washing Ashore (2000)
silk, linen, fiber reactive dyes, vat dye discharge
stitched, painted, printed
32.5 x 80cm (13 x 32")

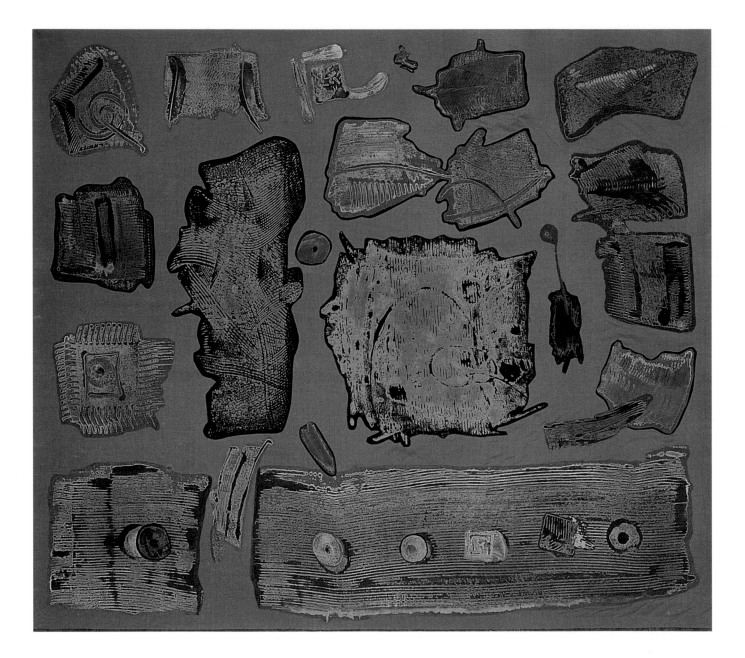

Dharma Light (1997)
silk, fiber reactive dyes, vat dye discharge
painted, printed
100 x 125cm (40 x 50")

Inanimate objects are thought to be without conscious awareness. Perhaps that is incorrect. These abstract forms have distinctive natures and are engaged in meaningful relationships.

Born   1941, New York City, New York

Education and Awards

1964	BFA, City College of New York
1966	MA in Painting, City College of New York
1987	Mid American Arts Alliance, NEA Grant
1992	First Prize from USA, Japan Fashion Foundation International Textile Design Competition
1992	IdeaComo (Italy), Award for Outstanding Achievement in Printed Textiles

Selected Exhibitions

2000	*Jason Pollen, Chance of Rain,* Dolphin Gallery, Kansas City, Missouri (solo)
2000	*Mining the Surface,* Temple Gallery, Philadelphia, Pennsylvania (solo)
2000	*Material Evidence,* Reed Whipple Cultural Center, Las Vegas, Nevada
1999	Snyderman Gallery, Philadelphia, Pennsylvania
1998	*Ten in Textiles,* Craft Alliance, St. Louis, Missouri
1997	*Threads,* New Jersey Center for the Visual Arts, Summit, New Jersey
1996	TextilMuseum Max Berk, Heidelberg, Germany
1995	*Silk Roads,* Roads of Contemporary Art, Lodz, Poland

Publications

1999	"Jason Pollen, Mining the Surface", *Surface Design Journal,* Winter Issue
1998	"Jason Pollen", *FIBERARTS,* Winter Issue
1997	"New Dimensions in Working with Fiber", William Zimmer, *New York Times*
1994	"Fragments in Composition", Janice T. Paine, *American Craft Magazine,* June/July

Professional

2000-	Full Professor, Chair, Fiber Department, Kansas City Art Institute, Missouri
2000-	President, Surface Design Association, Kansas
2000-	Director, Kansas City Friends of Tibet
1975-2000	Textile Designer for: Liberty of London, Jack Lenor Larsen, Lanvin, Yves St. Laurent, Jim Thompson Thai Silks, Wamsutta, PerryEllis, Printmaker International, Ungaro, Hallmark Cards Inc. and others

Work in Public Collections

Kemper Museum of Contemporary Art, Kansas City, Missouri
H & R Bloch International Headquarters, Kansas City, Missouri
Perry, Falkowski and Perry, Philadelphia, Pennsylvania
Printmaker International, New York

Kyoung Ae Cho

The linear forms of my work evolve out of my visual and sensual conversations with nature. I see my work almost as a ceremony, where a celebration of nature is transformed into a new birth, a new formal existence.

left:
Chaos II (1998) (detail)
wood, nails, paint
305 x 305cm (122 x 122")

right:
Portrait IV (1991)
honey locust stems, beeswax, hair
34.5 x 37 x 8.9cm (14 x 15 x 3½")

Traditionally in Korea the eldest son takes care of his parents and both my grandfather and my father were the eldest. Sadly, I knew neither my great grandfather nor my grandfather, but I did share a room with both my great grandmother and grandmother when I was growing up. Never having gone to school, my grandmother was not able to read and write, but she was a very talented sewer. She invented her own way of keeping records and had a wonderful memory. The Korean War meant her life was hard. She would collect things and turn them into beautiful objects which she would give away as presents. That was her pleasure in life. When I was very young she taught me how to sew and the importance of craftsmanship. She taught me to respect materials and above all I learnt that if you make anything with your heart the smallest thing can become something very special. These lessons still play an important part in my life.

I work with nature to express myself. All my childhood stories represent nature as a friend and a helper. For me it has personality as well as language, whether it is shape, pattern, color, texture, or anything affecting the senses. My works are concerned with the search for this common language.

During my graduate study I started to work with trees and other natural materials. I thought that if I could understand a small twig, I would be able to understand branches, and after that I would be able to understand a tree, and eventually I would be able to understand nature itself. Gathering materials is a very important part of my work. It is rather a ceremonial time when I have a conversation with the materials I find. I often describe my work as a 'collaboration' between nature and me; a movement to the next life.

I worked in my tiny bedroom for many years. One day, as I was cleaning, I rediscovered the beauty of one of my hairs. So I started to collect my hair and to use it as an element in my drawing and this led to *Portrait IV. Feather* is a piece made combining feathers and my hair. I have also worked with wire and hair to wrap gathered branches and stems. Throughout my work I have remained interested in line, particularly a line that has its own energy. My hair has been long almost all my life; it has been like a toy, and maybe that's where my fondness of linear elements comes from.

Pine Ball II (1996)
pine needles and burn marks on wood
89 x 115 x 115mm (3½ x 4½ x 4½")

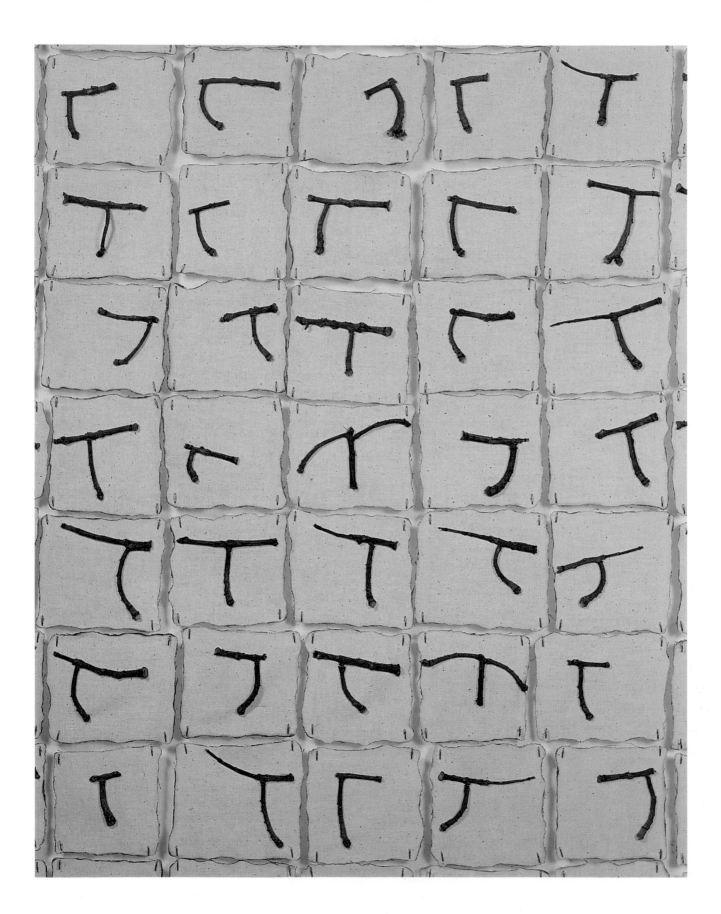

Living in an environment of such plenty, I feel the value of many things around us is overlooked. Many people in the US celebrate Christmas. I had always thought how ironic it was that people cut down trees just for one or two weeks to celebrate the birth of Jesus Christ. One year I dragged six or seven abandoned trees into my place thinking I could maybe extend their life. By recycling (mostly natural) materials I hope that I can provide one more chance for us to appreciate nature as well as recycled materials. *Evergreen Window* is my first piece from those Christmas trees. By putting needles inside a window frame, found in an abandoned house in Detroit, I was thinking of hope. From then on much of my work has been an exploration of those Christmas tree needles. By re-joining them to the wood I have, I hope, given them a new life. I also started to incorporate burn marks to celebrate the past life of the wood.

I became interested in the quilt (blanket) as the first 'architecture' one deals with in life. The relationship between tree and quilt interested me. In autumn a tree sheds its leaves and covers the ground, nurturing the earth for the next generation. Useless rags have often been collected and combined to make beautiful quilts handed down to the next generation with love and care. Because of their softness and strong grain, pine and fir are regarded as low-quality lumber. The weakness of the pine became a strength as I cross cut the timbers and put them together to make my quilt pieces including *Aged, Covered by Wisdom*, and *Quilt?I – I-V*. In this way I was able to combine my love of wood and my love of sewing.

As the earth lives and breathes, life is in a constant state of rebirth. In my work I transform found or man-made objects, adapting and reconstructing them into their next level of existence – in the environments where I place them. As part of this process I record their history as well as make new markings and shapes. Nature records both its past evolutions and insights into the future. Ultimately, these pieces are created through conversations with nature which have given me the four insights embedded in my works: Change, Time, Essence, Rebirth.

I am interested in the relationship between order and chaos. As nature is constantly adapting to its environment, it searches to survive. As a part of this incredible organization I approach my work and my life hoping to be able to understand its mysterious rhythm and rule that we only understand as chaos.

I was hoping that if I could understand a small twig, I would be able to understand branches, and after that I would be able to understand trees. And in the long run I might be able to understand nature itself.

We (1990) (detail)
chestnut twigs, pins, cotton, thread, burn marks
122 x 122 x 4cm (49 x 49 x 1½")

Evergreen Window (1993)
balsam fir needles,
window frame
85 x 55cm (34 x 22")

Born   1963, Onyang, South Korea

Education and Awards

1982-86	BFA, Duksung Women's University, South Korea
1989-91	MFA, Cranbrook Academy of Art, Michigan
1992	Art on the Move Grant, Detroit Recreation Department
1995	Grant, The Pollock-Krasner Foundation, Inc.
1997	Award of Excellence, Quilt National 1997
1997	The Lillian Elliott Award

Selected Exhibitions

1999	*Accumulation of Nature,* Paul Wieghardt Gallery, Evanston Art Center, Evanston, Illinois (solo)
1999	*The Practiced Hand; Constructions & Sculptural Fiber,* South Bend Regional Museum of Art, South Bend, Indiana
1999	*En Response,* The Writer's Place, Kansas City, Missouri
1998	*Modus Operandi, A Survey of Contemporary Fiber,* Snyderman/Works Galleries, Philadelphia, Pennsylvania
1998	*Perspective: Kansas City,* Gallery of Art, Johnson County Community College, Overland Park, Kansas
1998	*Rearrangements,* Kemper Museum of Contemporary Art, Kansas City, Missouri (solo)
1998	*The Branch, The Leaf,* Sheehan Gallery, Whitman College, Walla Walla, Washington (solo)
1997-99	*Quilt National 1997,* Dairy Barn Southeastern Ohio Cultural Arts Center, Athens, Ohio (tour)
1997	*But...Is it Quilt?,* Connell Gallery, Atlanta, Georgia
1997	*Fiber '97,* Textile Arts Center, Chicago, Illinois
1997	*What's in the Air, Young American Textile Artists,* Kansas City Artists Coalition, Kansas City, Missouri
1997	*Sense of Order,* Kansas City Artists Coalition, Kansas City, Missouri (solo)
1997	*Kyoung Ae Cho,* Urban Institute for Contemporary Arts, Grand Rapids, Michigan (solo)
1996	*4 Tangents,* el dorado inc., Kansas City, Missouri
1995	*Material Poetry,* The Katherine E. Nash Gallery, University of Minnesota, Minnesota
1995	*Interventions,* Detroit Institute of Arts, Detroit, Michigan
1995	*Quantitative Interpretation,* Paint Creek Center for the Arts, Rochester, Michigan (solo)
1994	*The Inner Spirit,* Sybaris Gallery, Royal Oak, Michigan
1993	*Pushing the Boundaries: Explorations in Fiber,* Evanston Art Center, Evanston, Illinois
1989	*The Fiber Miniature '89: A Show of Hands,* Carnegie Art Museum of Oxnard, Oxnard, California
1986	*86 Korean Craft Exhibition,* National Museum of Modern Art, Kwachon, South Korea

Professional

1999	Assistant Professor, University of Wisconsin-Milwaukee, Milwaukee, Wisconsin
1995-99	Instructor, Kansas City Art Institute, Kansas City, Missouri

There is something very sad about the wastefulness of Christmas trees being thrown out in a land of such plenty. By collecting their branches and arranging some needles inside this old window frame, I offer one more chance for us to appreciate nature – I am offering hope.

Charlene Nemec-Kessel

**My narratives record the life I observe around me.
However, just as stories go through a metamorphosis
each time they are told, mine evolve during the weaving.**

left:
Thousand Eyes of God (1999)
double weave pick-up and embroidery
rayon and cotton
76 x 54cm (30½ x 21½")

right:
Pauline's Garden (1996)
hand-woven voided velvet and embroidery
rayon and cotton thread
28 x 28cm (11 x 11½")

At the start of my education as an artist I discovered that most of my peers came from a very different world to mine. Having a working class background, I find it much easier to identify with the worker/weaver than with the elite of the art world. While the great tapestries of the late Middle Ages and Renaissance were designed by artists, they were woven by anonymous workers. By weaving stories from my own life, I want to validate those weavers' experiences. I wish to claim a craft that throughout time has been relegated to the working class.

My narratives record the life I observe around me. However, just as stories go through a metamorphosis each time they are told, mine evolve during the weaving. My repetition of stories during the painstaking processes of weaving and embroidery transforms them and while they have their origins in personal experience, they are not purely autobiographical. The changes in the tale are significant. They reveal what the teller needs to say, and because he or she responds to what listeners want to hear, the changes also reveal something about the listeners. Perhaps these fictions speak more honestly about a life or a culture at a particular point in time than any factual report ever could.

I use both pattern and image to record my stories. My intention is to challenge the subordination of pattern in Western art. I surround image with pattern, putting both on equal ground. The pattern does not function simply as a frame, but it is essential to the narrative. In *Merciless Chirping*, two women are frozen in conversation. The pattern of repeated birds in the border is broken as one bird pecks out its companion's eye. By reducing the central image and enlarging the border I further accentuate the validity of the decorative arts in relation to Western fine art.

Many of the late Medieval and Renaissance tapestries are laden with symbols. I draw on that language, knowing that few people today recognize the traditional meanings of the symbols, which, in themselves, are also open to many interpretations. These layers of meaning are an integral part of my work.

The pattern in *Pins and Needles* consists of a woman picking up a pair of scissors and putting them down again. The action is repeated endlessly, perhaps suggesting the routine of traditional 'women's work'.

The motif the woman inhabits resembles the female reproductive system, implying the mother-daughter relationship and the transmission of tradition from generation to generation. However, the woman holds a pair of scissors, the tool used to sever this connection. The woman could also be sitting in a hand held fan, a traditional symbol of unfolding life. Being a purely feminine object, the fan is often seen as seductive; so paired with a woman holding scissors may imply a *femme fatale*.

This is emphasized by the intersection of the image and pattern. A woman towers above a man who is held by a rope to the tree he is cutting down. Because of the scale of the image and the pattern, the rope appears as a delicate thread that could easily be snipped by the woman.

The pattern in *Pins and Needles* consists of a woman picking up a pair of scissors and putting them down again. The action is repeated endlessly, perhaps suggesting the routine of traditional 'women's work'.

The motif the woman inhabits resembles the female reproductive system, implying the mother-daughter relationship and the transmission of tradition from generation to generation. However, the woman holds a pair of scissors, the tool used to sever this connection. The woman could also be sitting in a hand held fan, a traditional symbol of unfolding life. Being a purely feminine object, the fan is often seen as seductive; so paired with a woman holding scissors may imply a *femme fatale*...

Pins and Needles (1996)
double-weave pick-up and embroidery
rayon, cotton and silk thread
50 x 50cm (20 x 20")

However, a fan can also be seen as an object of submission; as in a ruler being fanned by his harem. The autumn fan symbolizes an abandoned wife. The woman is perched on the tree the man is cutting down, but the tree is part of nature, which has so long been associated with women. There is a constant power-play between male and female throughout the weaving. The pincushion in the foreground is another purely feminine object, but it is pierced with pins. Although suggesting self-destruction, the pincushion's attitude seems to coyly imply that she is completely in charge.

The pattern motif could also be interpreted as a hand mirror. Mirrors are associated with the function of art – a reflection of society. In the fairy tale Snow White a mirror speaks absolute truth. In *Alice Through the Looking Glass* a mirror is an entrance into a parallel world. Although seeming to reflect the world exactly, reflected images in mirrors are actually reversed.

The border of *Binomial* is filled with split pineapples. The pineapple is a symbol of hospitality, but the fiery motif also resembles a falling bomb. The pattern is cut off in mid-pineapple, and the woman's companion in the central image is clipped from view. I intentionally crop both the pattern and the image so what the viewer sees is a fragment of something that is never ending.

I have recently started work on a series of beaded peyote stitch containers, which are intended to be shown in conjunction with my weavings. A few of the vessels are constructed entirely of beads and thread, but most also have inset areas of tapestry and embroidery. Each box will contain one of my written short stories, tales created during the hours I spend doing the meticulous needlework. The images and pattern worked into the container are related to the written story held within it.

Some containers I have made were inspired by the embroidered caskets that young women made in seventeenth century England. Used to store writing implements, toilet articles and other personal items, the caskets sometimes had secret compartments. They were covered in elaborately embroidered narratives, using thread, beads, hair, feather and bits of mica. Embroidery was one of the few pastimes considered appropriate for a 'proper' young woman. Throughout history there has been a notion that "idle hands are the devil's workshop", but one wonders what the young women thought about in those hours of monotonous handwork. The stories in my containers, which often contain rather 'improper' scenes, challenge the traditional associations of domestic embroidery.

I am committed to telling the stories of those who don't often have a voice in the art world; not only the working class, but also the female experience. Women are heard much more today, but I explore the life of the female isolated in the home and the embroidery tradition is the perfect vehicle for telling her tale.

My tapestries and beaded containers record stories that might otherwise go unnoticed. I keep my eyes and ears open; I gather images and stories as I go about my day. Eventually these bits and pieces are rearranged and shuffled until they are transformed into something that preserves the integrity of the original while saying something more than the fragments alone can say.

The pineapple is a symbol of hospitality, but the fiery motif also resembles a falling bomb. The pattern is cut off in mid-pineapple: I intentionally crop both the pattern and the image, so what the viewer sees is a fragment of something that is never ending.

Binomial (1995)
triple weave pick-up and embroidery
rayon and cotton thread
74 x 53cm (29½ x 21")

Born   1970, Milwaukee, Wisconsin

Education and Awards

1989	Frances Hook National Merit Scholarship
1989-93	BA Fine Art (Merit Scholarship), The School of the Art Institute of Chicago
1993	Award for Excellence, Textile Art Center Exhibition, Chicago, Illinois
1993	Award for Excellence, New Art Forms juried exhibition, Coalition of Creative Organizations, Chicago, Illinois
1995	Honorable Mention Award, Florida National Combined Talents, Tallahassee, Florida
1995-97	MA Fine Art (Merit Scholarship), The School of the Art Institute of Chicago
1997	James Nelson Raymond Fellowship
1997	Award for Excellence, Expressions of Culture national juried exhibition, SOFA, Chicago, Illinois

Selected Exhibitions

1999	Lyons Wier Gallery, Chicago, Illinois (solo)
1999	*Expressions in Fiber,* Evanston Art Center, Evanston, Illinois (solo)
1998	SOFA, New York, represented by Lyons Wier Gallery, Chicago, Illinois
1997	SOFA, Chicago 1997, Expressions of Culture national juried exhibition
1997	*Figurative Influences in Clay and Fiber,* New Bedford Art Museum, New Bedford, Massachusetts
1997	*Mentors as Makers,* Textile Arts Center, Chicago, Illinois
1997	*Soft,* H20 Gallery, Milwaukee, Wisconsin
1996	*New Voices in Weaving,* Contemporary Crafts Gallery, Portland, Oregon
1994, 95	*Florida National Combined Talents,* Florida State University Museum of Fine Arts, Tallahassee, Florida
1994	*Currents '94,* Lill Street Gallery, Chicago, Illinois
1993, 94	*Chatauqua International for Fiber Art,* Adams Art Gallery, Dunkirk, New York
1993	*New Talent,* Contemporary Art Workshop, Chicago, Illinois
1993	Textile Arts Center Exhibition, Chicago, Illinois
1993	New Art Forms juried exhibition, Coalition of Creative Organizations, Chicago, Illinois

Professional

1997-98	Associate Lecturer, Fiber Art, University of Wisconsin, Milwaukee
1997-98	Associate Lecturer, Fiber Art and Design, Concordia University, Mequon, Wisconsin

Publications

1998	"Deceptive Ornament", Barbara Lee Smith, *Surface Design Journal,* Winter Issue
1998	"Looking for Intimacy in all the Wrong places", Margo Mensing, *FIBERARTS,* Summer Issue

Devour (1999)
double weave pick-up and embroidery
rayon and cotton thread
87 x 56cm (34⅜ x 22")

I use both pattern and image to record my stories. My intention is to challenge the subordination of pattern in Western art. I surround image with pattern, putting both on equal ground. The pattern does not function simply as a frame, but it is essential to the narrative.

Jane Sauer

I want my work to communicate the delicate balance of all human relationships. In *Tender Moments* I want to express that moment when a mother must release a young adult into the world and yet feels all the urges to hold close and protect. The mother and child have the conflict of enjoying their present relationship but knowing it must change in order to grow.

left:
Tender Moments (1996)
knotted waxed linen threads, acrylic paint
60 x 55 x 27.5cm (24 x 22 x 11")

right:
Continuum (1997)
knotted waxed linen threads, acrylic paint
36.25 x 117.5cm diameter (14½ x 47")

I was born in 1937 in St.Louis, Missouri. From the time I was about 5 years old, I believed I was an artist. My father, a doctor, told me that one of his examining rooms was my studio and I would come there every day after school. He placed my drawings and paintings around his office and my work was praised by his patients and staff. I was very fortunate to grow up believing creativity was a part of everyday life.

I attended Washington University School of Fine Arts. My training was in painting although my passion was to make objects. Sculpture in the 1950s was a male dominated field and other disciplines did not have the status of 'fine art' and were not taught in such depth.

In the early years, after college, I earned an income with several art-related jobs. I was unable to work in a studio and sell what I produced, although I was always creating something. When I didn't have a space I used a bedroom, a kitchen, the basement, and eventually converted a dining room to a work studio. I had always wanted to express myself with my hands.

I also had the experience of looking after seven small children before I could seriously begin a career as an artist. Once I found time to experiment, it was with ideas, materials and techniques. In the 1970s basket making was just entering the new and experimental textile movement. I found the technique of knotting threads by accident, in a 'how to do' book, and taught myself the process. Without a teacher, I found my own answers to technical problems. Although this was laborious at times, it meant that I didn't have to unlearn a process to find new solutions. I made up many ways of using this technique as my work became more challenging. Making baskets by this slow intensive method meets some obsessive need I have to build forms by interlocking small elements. I truly enjoy creating a structure in this way. The deliberate building, knot by knot, gives me time to contemplate, and allows me to be intimately involved with the manipulation of the waxy silky thread.

After an idea has been formed, I make a number of preliminary drawings. I enjoy this process and occasionally the drawing will become an end in itself, though usually it is only a method of pinning down the form I see in my mind's eye. Once I feel satisfied with the general shape and gesture, I begin carving a large block of styrofoam, shaping it with knives and files. It is then painted with as many as six coats of polymer and sanded to create a smooth hard surface on which I build a structure of knots.

The material used for knotting is waxed linen thread. I like the ability of fiber to be hard and soft, to be a linear element and to be able to construct a whole cloth. The color is always central to the idea, and is established in the drawing stage. Even if it is a colored linen, I am never satisfied with just one color. Therefore, before beginning to knot, I glaze or lightly paint the threads with acrylic paint. Although most of the painting takes place before the threads are used, I often paint during the building of the structure. The color can reflect the mood of the piece; the challenge for me is in combining the color and form to express my idea.

Ulibarri (1999)
waxed linen and pigment
132.5 x 23.75 x 8.75cm
(53 x 9½ x 3½")

The structure is made row upon row, using hundreds of thousands of half hitch knots. I view the ridges as lines moving around the form, supporting and elaborating on the nature of the shape, telling a story of expansion, contraction and tension.

My shapes have become progressively simpler and more sculptural as the message of the work has taken over. For many years I have been interested in the dynamics of human relationships. Being part of a large and fluid family, I am constantly trying to understand the nature of communication. I am amazed by the universality of certain emotions such as loneliness and isolation and the need to connect with a community, a partner or a friend. Power struggles are intriguing whether between parent and child or between partners, as within a marriage. I want my work to communicate the delicate balance of all human relationships. Many of my pieces consist of two or three parts placed in a specific relationship to each other. The empty space between the pieces is as important as the positive space. I want the whole to be stronger than each part. The shapes express tensions, contradictions and the interplay of the connections in life. My work deals with the specifics of my own life, but hopefully shares my experiences with a wider audience at the same time.

I often think about the struggle between chaos and order in my images. The structure is made row upon row, using hundreds of thousands of half hitch knots. I view the ridges as lines moving around the form, supporting and elaborating on the nature of the shape, telling a story of expansion, contraction and tension.

No Separation (1998)
waxed linen thread and paint
70 x 40.5 x 25.5cm (27½ x 16 x 10")

Born   1937, St. Louis, Missouri

Education and Awards

1959   BFA, Washington University, St. Louis, Missouri
1980   4th International Exhibit of Miniature Textiles, British Crafts Centre, London: 1st prize
1984, 90   National Endowment for the Arts Visual Artist Grant
1991   IN OUR HANDS, International Competition, Nagoya, Japan: Shinkol Award

Selected Exhibitions

1998   *Threads Contemporary American Basketry,* Barbican Centre, London, England
1997   R. Duane Reed Gallery, St. Louis, Missouri (solo)
1996   *Breaking the Barriers: Recent American Craft,* Portland Art Museum, Portland, Oregon (tour)
1996   *Fiber: Five Decades from the Permanent Collection,* American Craft Museum, New York City
1995   Nancy Margolis Gallery, New York City (solo)
1994   Okun Gallery, Santa Fe, New Mexico (solo)
1992   *15th Biennale Internationale de la Tapisserie,* Lausanne, Switzerland (tour Belgium)
1992   The Tactile Vessel, Erie Art Museum, Erie, Pennsylvania (tour)
1992   *Knots and Nets,* Johnson Museum of Art, Cornell University, Ithaca, New York
                (tour USA and Africa)
1988   St. Louis Art Museum, St. Louis, Missouri (solo)
1986   Craft Today: Poetry of the Physical, American Craft Museum, Inaugural Exhibit, New York
                (tour: USA, Europe and Russia through 1991)

Work in Public Collections

                American Craft Museum, New York City
                Arkansas Art Center Decorative Arts Museum, Little Rock, Arizona
                Detroit Institute of Arts, Detroit, Michigan
                Erie Art Museum, Erie, Pennsylvania
                M.H. de Young Museum, San Francisco, California
                Mint Museum, Charlotte, North Carolina
                Museum of Suwa, Japan
                Nordenfjeldske Kunstindustrimuseum, Tronndheim, Norway
                Philadelphia Museum of Art, Philadelphia, Pennsylvania
                St. Louis Art Museum, St. Louis, Missouri
                The Contemporary Museum of Art, Honolulu, Hawaii
                Wadsworth Atheneum, Hartford, Connecticut
                Washington University, St. Louis, Missouri
                Wustum Museum, Racine, Wisconsin

**All families have stories. Many stories centre around the desire
for interdependence and independence. Caregivers (mothers)
can become overwhelming in their desire to shelter and protect.
There is a struggle between these forces.**

Protection and Other Domestic Stories (1997)
knotted waxed linen threads, acrylic paint
92.5 x 31.25 x 36.25cm (37 x 12½ x 14½")

Deborah Fisher

My work is an intimate unfolding of stories that hover between nightmare and fairy tale. I work to reconcile this dichotomy. Become an escape artist, your own magician of circumstance.

Organ Wands (1995)
velvet, satin, plastic, wire, rattan, vinyl, found objects
61 x 71 x 51cm (24 x 28 x 20")

I often wonder why we make things. One spring a bird built a nest in our mailbox. Each day she would fly in and out through a gap in the warped door, constructing the nest out of twigs and string. Soon there were four speckled eggs inside and then four tiny birds. Then one day the birds flew away and we were left with the nest, a memento. It was a fantastic process. And it made me think more about my own work and the act of making.

Are we seeking a manifestation of creation? Dig a hole in the ground and plant a seed. Is making an expression of creation or just an imitation? The essential connections between the world, my work and my own self are continuously unfolding. Those connections become most visible to me when I am inspired by an old worn shoe sole washed onto the beach or daffodils dried on their stems in our garden. I find the most beautiful shell or stone and am speechless at the sight, but also speechless in the making, wondering how do I express that amazement, how do I capture that? How is universal humanity intertwined with our own personal mythology and history? What is important, what do you like, what are your afraid of, what is at the centre?

In my work, I have developed an intimate way of making, a meeting of mind with materials, and then a transforming. The process becomes a backstitch, a continuous thread; always going forward but sometimes taking a little from the past and that makes a stronger seam. All the objects, including latches and knobs, are made by hand. That presence of the maker is significant.

I often use the forms of tools and everyday objects, utilitarian as well as ceremonial. They are objects that we invent or discover. They spur the senses and serve as a beginning for investigation and discussion. Consider the essence of an object, the 'scissorness' of scissors, the 'weaponness' of a weapon. Objects can be surprisingly visionary. They imply possibility: a handle needs to be held. Likewise, a carrying case needs to be carried. We use boxes to hold our most precious belongings. They protect as well as reveal and conceal. The cigar box, the suitcase, Pandora's box. The theatrical stage set is a container where we create and present our own fictions.

In my daydreams I see a small boy with a box of nests on stick handles like candied apples. Each nest is made of something different like bark or wool or a curled leaf. The boy carries his box of nests into a field and picks a nest out of the box. He holds it, arm outstretched, and a bird comes to sit in it. I look inside his box and see the nests. But I could also see something else. I could see a secret or a jewel, a nightmare or a memory.

I work to create provocative and evocative situations that speak of a world beyond itself. A new metaphor. Small scale allows a connection from body to object, from mind to narrative. The objects may become like a story, the words enclosed in a small space between covers. They are like a hidden universe, revealing yet elemental. Enchanting possibilities can be created by bridging adulthood and childhood, culture and the natural world. Ordinary awareness turns into fanciful reverie. The connecting of fiction to reality becomes mythology.

What do you encounter in the dark, at night, or even in twilight? The beating of moth wings around a beckoning light, the scent of a mysterious hidden something, the glowing white flowers or stones that guide you? There are many definitions for dark. What are your fears?

Tools for if you are afraid of the dark (1998)
cotton and linen thread, wax, wood, wire, egg shells, natural and fragrant found objects
25 x 18 x 9cm (10 x 7 x 3½")

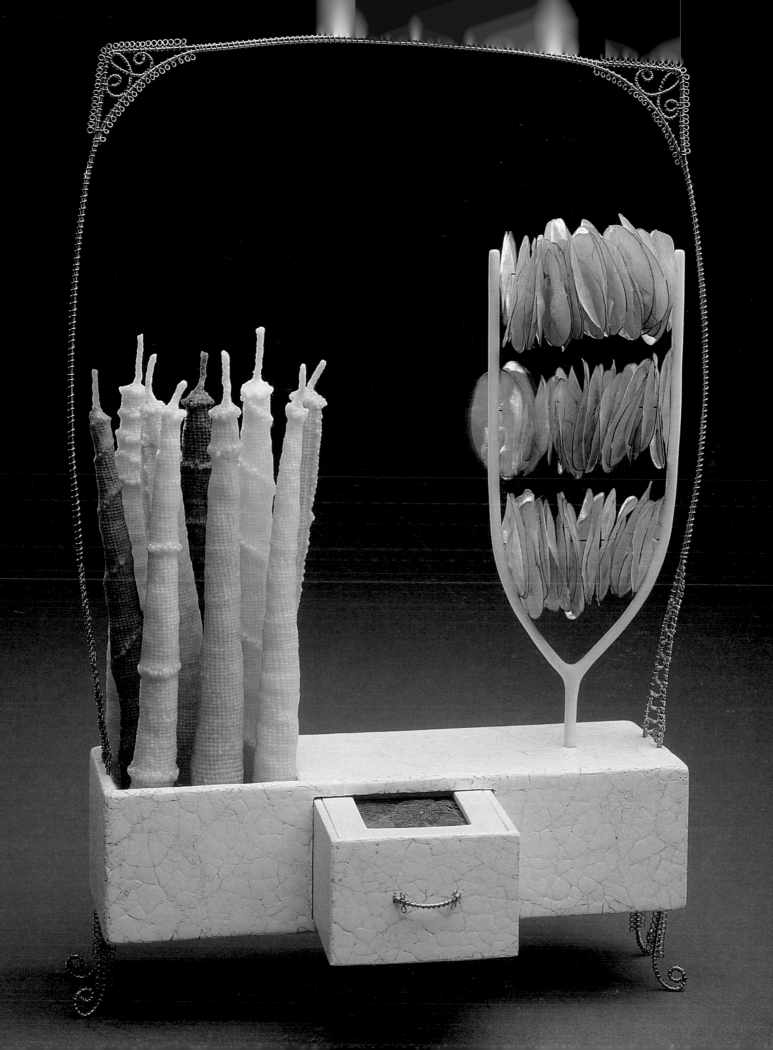

As artists we are sometimes told to separate ourselves from what we have made. But how can we when we are Dorothy in Oz? I wonder if I am simply the creator or if I fit into these worlds. Am I storyteller or character, puppeteer or marionette? While I work, I am a spider building a web but I am also a child playing with a dollhouse. Move the furniture; put the mother in the sink, put the baby under the bed and see what happens.

The work is always changing and I am surprised by each transformation. I want to invite curiosity and wonderment and hint at things just out of the ordinary. I want to create the sense that maybe it, whatever it is, could happen.

I do not make work for a larger audience. I make work for you, that one individual, with the small hope that it will reach out with a dangerous yet delicate touch to move you. I want to make objects that make you feel something in your gut, in your heart. I want to magnify and expound what is beautiful, what is painful, what is aching, what is magical. I want to make it real and make it unreal. It is an expanding mystery. We capture one and another comes into being, revealing itself like a veiled bride, or the ground coming through melted snow. Recover and uncover to reveal something new.

I see my grandmother sewing our family together with a continuous thread, with backstitches. This is the same with the process of making. Always going forward but sometimes taking a little from the past and that makes a stronger seam.

I can still see you, Grandma (1994)
reed, linen, silk, wood, latex, hair,
found objects, silver leaf
31 x 31 x 41cm (12 x 12 x 16")

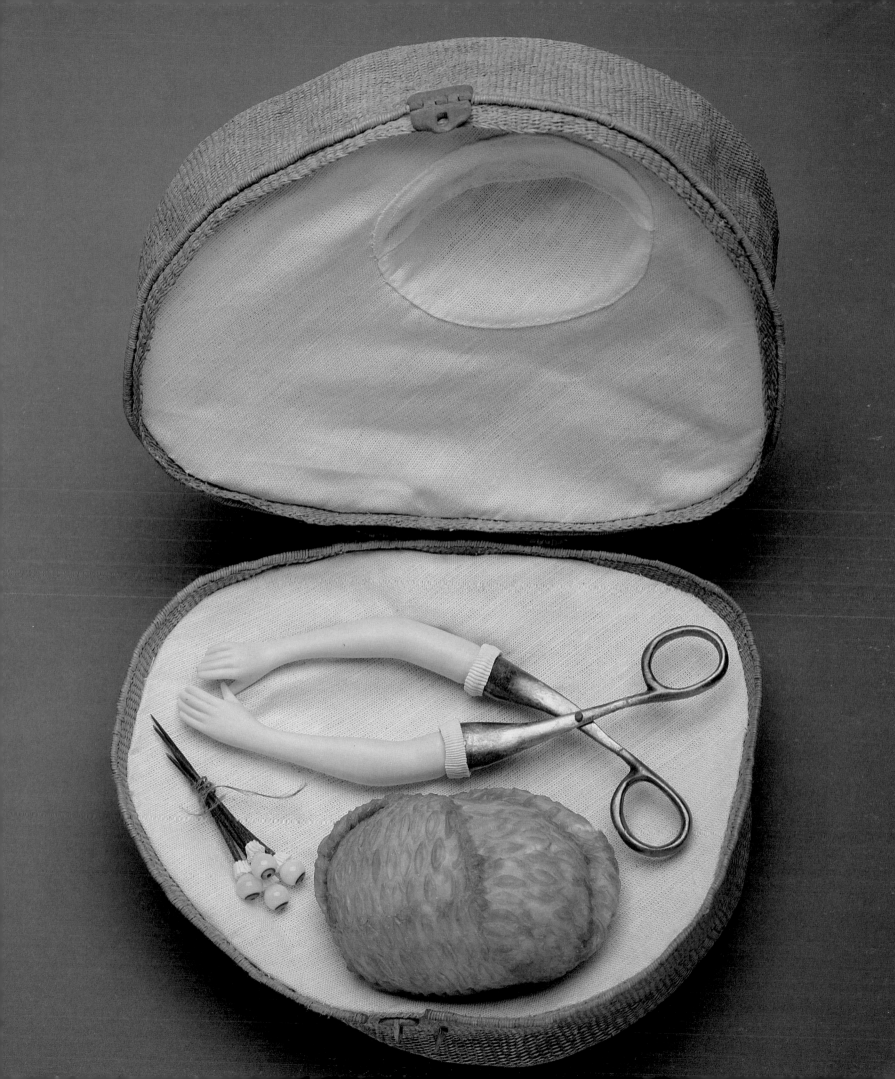

I make work for you, that one individual, with the small hope that it will reach out with a dangerous yet delicate touch to move you. I want to make objects that make you feel something in your gut, in your heart. I want to magnify and expound what is beautiful, what is painful, what is aching, what is magical.

In my mind I'm dancing (2000)
wood, cotton, linen, silk, vinyl,
copper wire, found objects
109 x 46 x 122cm (43 x 18 x 48")

Born   1970, Lynchburg, Virginia

Education and Awards

1992   BFA Fiber, Maryland Institute, College of Art, Baltimore, Maryland
1997   New York Foundation for the Arts Artists' Fellowship
1999   DeRoy Award
2000   Nita "Billie" Barak Memorial Scholarship
2001   MFA Fiber, Cranbrook Academy of Art, Michigan

Selected Exhibitions

1999   *Beneath the Skin: Recent work by Deborah Fisher and James Fischetti,*
         Heckscher Museum of Art at Bryant Library, Roslyn, New York
1998   *20/XX: An Invitational Exhibition of XX Alumni Artists from the Last 20 Years,*
         Meyerhoff Gallery, Maryland Institute, College of Art, Baltimore, Maryland
1998   *Untitled:* Deborah Fisher, Jane A. Herrick, Paulette Singer, Anthony Giordano Gallery,
         Oakdale, New York
1998   *Rip Shrink Cut or Stitch: Appreciating Fiber Art,* WPA/Corcoran Projectspace, Washington, DC
1997   *Deborah Fisher, Lisa Lawley, Harvey Quaytman, Alice Vitali,* Art Awareness Gallery,
         Lexington, New York
1997   *Wands and Tools,* The Cecelia Coker Bell Gallery, Hartsville, South Carolina (solo)
1994   *Materials: Hard and Soft,* Meadows Gallery at the Center for Visual Arts, Denton, Texas
1994   *Eye to Eye: Artists Invite Artists,* The Graphic Eye Gallery, Port Washington, New York
1993   *Botanics,* Gallery Ten, Rockford, Illinois
1993   *Vessels,* The Upper Gallery, Milwaukee, Wisconsin
1993   *The Domestic Object: Articles for Everyday Living,* The Berkshire Museum,
         Pittsfield, Massachusetts
1993   *And the Women Danced,* Borowsky Gallery at the Gershman Y, Philadelphia, Pennsylvania
1993   *Exhibition 280: Works Off Walls,* Huntington Museum of Art, Huntington, West Virginia
1992   *Just Plane Screwy: Metaphysical and Metaphorical Tools by Artists,*
         Charles A. Wustum Museum of Fine Arts, Racine, Wisconsin

Virginia Davis

DAVIS, VIRGINIA
Ceci n'est pas une diapositive.
54cm×49cm: Technique personelle

AOUT94

left:
Whitescape (1998)
linen, bleach, dye
double ikat
91 x 74cm (36 x 29")

right:
This is not a Slide (1994)
oil, acrylic, nail polish, computer printer collage
handwoven ikat linen canvas
88 x 88cm (35 x 35")

My work challenges definitions of what constitutes art, and brings into focus questions about the nature of the alleged hierarchy of media and techniques and does so in a manner that challenges established prejudice.

It was a revealing experience for me to be told at an art supply store that a scrap of my hand-woven linen was exactly like their finest Belgian painters canvas. I saw that by weaving linen canvas, similar to that used by traditional artists, I could lead viewers to challenge old definitions of what constitutes art. In my studio I keep swatches of canvas from various art supply stores and use these as models for the weaving structure of my 'canvases'. Ikat technique, directly dyeing or painting the image on the threads before weaving, enables color and image to be embedded in the woven structure and locked inside the canvas. In this manner, I comment on the materials of art, referring to the 16th-century transition from images in fresco (or on wood) to painting on fabric. Thus woven linen cloth became a conventional support for the image which, in my interpretation, moves inside the canvas as a deconstructed painting. The message is the metaphoric removal of the divide between the crafts and fine arts.

Formally, the work explores aspects of vision and nuances of contrast. Color reflects light differently depending on whether it is placed in the warp or weft. The representation of space occurs through color overlay. There is a play of edge, hard and feathered; theme and variation interact and cumulate, resulting in a meditative feeling. The work shows the beauty and subtleties inherent in the structure of textiles.

I did not start out as a weaver. In fact, I began my artistic studies with sculpture in London and New York. The formal training I received was in the traditional subtractive techniques of sculpture in stone and wood. In the late 1960s and early 1970s there was a lot of work around which combined pliable elements such as plastic tubing or rope. A fellow student at the Art Students League in New York told me of the Riverside Arts and Crafts School, where she thought there was a course in rope making. I was interested, although when I went to enroll I discovered that the course was mostly about dyeing and spinning. I decided to sign up anyway, and found myself two years later with a huge amount of handspun yarn dyed in vegetable colors and indigo.

I later studied under Sandra Harner, herself a student of Ed Rossbach's at the University of California. She showed me how to tie-dye patterns onto my yarns before weaving them into a textile. I was captivated by this method of controlling pattern and color, and my first ikats were made as a result.

Since then I have tried to learn as much as possible about similar processes from different cultures. I've studied Indian and Mexican resist techniques, for example, and in the 1970s at Berkeley I learnt Japanese *kasuri* techniques with Yoshiko Wada and Jun Tomita. In Jun's workshop I made a particular study of *e-gasuri*. This is a very refined, elaborate, and labour-intensive technique for producing a picture in the weaving. Jun often said "you'll never finish, there is too much tying". But I would pretend to leave at the end of the day and sneak back in before the class began. In this way I finished the tying and was rewarded by seeing the image emerge in the weaving. Under the influence of the Japanese tradition, I continued to work in silk dyed with indigo. My piece *Sky Curtain* produces the illusion of dimensional drapery by means of value contrast and non-alignment of lines.

Beneath the Surface (1998) (detail)
linen, hologram
double weave, painted warp
22 x 22 x 9cm (8½ x 8½ x 3½")

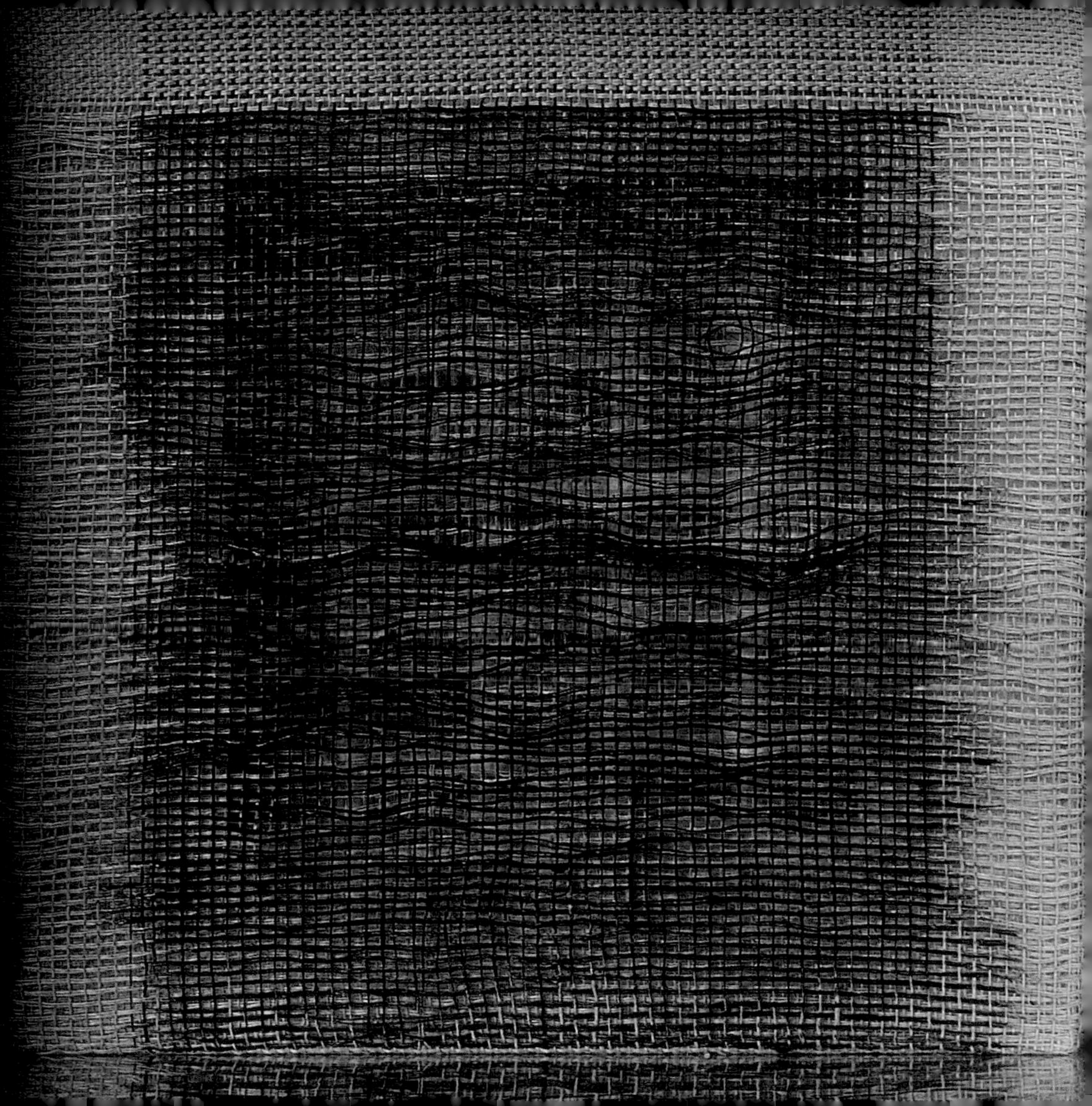

Although I found silk interesting and rewarding, I was eager to move in other directions. That was how I began experimenting with fine linen yarn. At first I restricted myself to black, white and grey values. The *Log Cabin* series is an exercise in the change of scale in patterning. But it is not only a play on a popular quilt block pattern with that name; it also refers to a color and weave technique nicknamed 'log cabin' by weavers. In my *Tartan* series I used a wider color palette, so the green tartan which began this series has the color structure and the 2/2 twill of the Davidson clan tartan. In an abstract sense it could be seen as an interpretation of a color field study. From a 1990s perspective, my work examines the idea of minimalism in textile imagery.

For an artist, attending to the way material and technique influence the process is, of course, essential. But my intention is to produce work that will speak to viewers with little or no knowledge of these technicalities. I see my pieces as image driven with several layers of meaning. In my most recent work, the symbolic significance of material plays an increasing role. In one direction, with linen canvas the basic field, I am incorporating a layering of surfaces, e.g. oil painting on the surface and using materials such as paper and plastic. In addition, one of my current aims is a woven amalgam of text and textile imagery. Satire is another element I have tried to incorporate in recent pieces. I believe my work challenges definitions of what constitutes art, and brings into focus questions about the nature of the alleged hierarchy of media and techniques, and does so in a manner that challenges established prejudice. My texts are chosen to provoke thought. Since the core meaning in my work began to evolve over fifteen years ago, it is gratifying that not only are the ideas being grasped, but that there is much more to be said.

**The misalignment of the checks
shows that the mend is all too visible.**

The Invisible Mend (1995)
linen, pigment
double ikat technique
91 x 91cm (36 x 36")

The technique, words in weft ikat, is a result of my stay in Orissa in East India, where sacred texts from the Gita Govinda are woven in this technique. The form, a scroll, comes from a trip to Prague, where the sacred scrolls in the Jewish Museum made a lasting impression on me.

Scroll (1994)
linen, indigo cotton backing
weft ikat
270 x 45cm (116½ x 17½")

Born   1929, Kansas City, Missouri

Education and Awards

1946-50	BA Sociology, Smith College of New York
1950-53	MA Sociology, University of Illinois
1968-69	Sir John Cass College of Art, London
1969-72	Art Students League, New York
1971-72	Riverside School of Arts and Crafts, New York
1974,76-77,78-79	Fiberworks, Berkeley, California
1982-83	National Endowment for the Arts Visual Artists Fellowship Grant
1988	New York State Foundation for the Arts Fellowship Grant
1989	3rd Annual MITI Textile Design Contest, Tokyo (semi-finalist)
1989	American Handweavers Competition (honorable mention)
1990-91	Indo-American Fellowship
1992-93	National Endowment for the Arts Visual Artists Fellowship Grant
1994	US/France International Artist Fellowship at *Cité Internationale des Arts*
1995	New York State Foundation for the Arts Fellowship Grant
1995	US/Mexico International Artist Fellowship (NFA/FONCA)

Selected Exhibitions

1998	*Webs/Textiles & New Technology,* University of California
1998	*Weaving Metaphors,* Arts Benicia Center Gallery, Benicia, California (three persons)
1998	*9 x 9 x 3,* American Craft Museum, New York
1997	*Looking Backwards/Forwards,* Textile Art Center, Chicago (solo)
1996	*Synergy,* Littman Gallery, Portland State University, Portland, Oregon
1996	*Order, System, Structure,* Rensselaer County Arts Center, Troy, New York (three persons)
1996	*Visiting Artists Jacquard Project,* Paley Design Center, Philadelphia College of Textiles
1995	*New Directions '95,* Barrett House Galleries, Poughkeepsie, New York
1995	*Conceptual Textiles,* Invitational, Kohler Arts Center, Sheboygan, Wisconsin
1995	*Thread Bare,* SE Center for Contemporary Art, Winston-Salem, North Carolina
1995	*Fast Forward,* Contemporary Gallery, Museum for Textiles, Toronto (solo)
1992	*9th International Minitextile Biennial,* Savaria Museum, Szombathely, Hungary
1987	*13th Biennale Internationale de la Tapisserie,* Lausanne, Switzerland
1986	*Virginia Davis,* Gayle Willson Gallery, Southampton, New York (solo)

Linda Hutchins

left:
DO NOT CROSS THIS LINE (1994) (detail)
woven tapestry (cotton), metal stands
tapestry strip: 7.5cm x 18m (3" x 60ft)

right:
Hurdles (1996)
woven tapestry (cotton), metal stands
(model – figure included for scale only)
60 x 180 x 120cm (2 x 6 x 4ft)

My tapestry installations are subversive and confrontational. They are surprisingly easily mistaken for actual barricades and have been obeyed, ignored, or even stepped on. They satirize the artistic hierarchies that separate, say, a bath towel, the *Bayeux Tapestry* and Warhol's *Brillo Box*.

Propriety, conformity and confinement are issues that run through all of my work. They have propelled me from my beginnings in tapestry to my current mixed-media sculptural approach. Since relinquishing tapestry, structure, materials and ordinary objects have taken on a much greater significance in my work.

I learnt textile techniques as a child. My mother hoped to be an artist, achieving a BA in design before settling into marriage and motherhood. My father is an engineer, and expert in sailing and fine craftsmanship. From them I learnt embroidery, sewing, knitting, crochet and knot-tying. I learnt to weave at the local 'Y', and discovered textile artists – Neda Al-Hilali, Aurelia Muñoz and Claire Zeisler – from my macramé books. From an early age I wanted to make images in fabric. I had the notion that an image woven or knotted into the structure of a fabric had more integrity than one printed, painted or embroidered on the surface. I wanted the image to be made as the fabric was made, not applied later. This ideal of a constructed image drew me to tapestry, as much as any sensual appeal of color or texture.

Before going to art school, I received a Bachelor's degree in computer engineering and worked for five years as a software engineer. I see a lot in common between engineering and art making. As an artist, I still see things as problems to be solved, and search for cohesive solutions.

While an engineer, I studied weaving at evening classes and workshops. To challenge my love of fibers, I deliberately chose an art school with no textile program at all. Despite the possibility of being seduced by another medium, my interest in tapestry survived.

In my early work, I relished the process of translating my drawings and paintings into weaving. It wasn't until the birth of my son in 1990 that I began to question not only the time commitment involved but also the separation of designing from making tapestry. What began as a conversation with the medium became an argument. I needed to come to terms with what defines tapestry and what compelled me to make it. For a while, tapestry's restrictions and demands provided a means of expressing the sense of confinement I felt in life and the demands I placed on myself as wife, mother, artist and woman. My struggle with tapestry mirrored my personal struggle. But when the argument intensified, and the tapestry became my adversary as much as my accomplice, I had to dispense with it and find a new way of working.

Facing South (not shown) is an early attempt to escape the confines of tapestry through a more spontaneous approach to design and execution; the elements of the composition were selected intuitively as I went along. I thought of the long narrow strip as a literal record of the passage of time, like a core sample extracted from the earth. *Facing South* hints at my growing obsession with the structural qualities of tapestry: the discrete point of weft over warp, the separation of one shape from another, the real, physical edge of a slit, the linear growth of the weaving itself. Tapestry's inherent structure is a manifestation of confinement and propriety, themes that are central to my work.

Wrapping bread in bailing wire is an act of binding, an attempt to restrain it, to better grasp its meaning. But just as barricade tape doesn't physically restrain anyone, wire can't really contain the bread. The slices are dry and brittle. Chunks keep crumbling off.

Three Ways (1999)
wire, sliced white bread
12.5 x 36.25 x 28.75cm
(5 x 14½ x 11½")

In *DO NOT CROSS THIS LINE*, I could no longer ignore the constraints imposed by the tapestry medium. While I love tapestry's structure, I questioned its manifestation as a big picture hanging on a wall. I wanted to challenge the lines between craft and art, tapestry and textile, art object and everyday object. I wanted my work to be conceptual and confrontational, to compete with real things in real space. More than making images, I wanted to make objects.

I used barricade tape to make the point. The absurdity of weaving this long strip allowed me to dismiss all sense of propriety and get on with it. Who ever heard of weaving a tapestry so completely predetermined, down to every last point of weft over warp? Who ever heard of executing tapestry like counted cross-stitch? While following the definition of tapestry to the letter, *DO NOT CROSS THIS LINE* subverts its spirit. It is tapestry that isn't tapestry. Stretched between stanchions as a free-standing installation, it is surprisingly easily mistaken for an actual barricade tape. The piece is obeyed, ignored, or even stepped on. It satirizes the artistic hierarchies that separate, say, a bath towel, the *Bayeux Tapestry* and Warhol's *Brillo Box*.

Hurdles is a direct response to my growing awareness that the tapestry medium itself can be a hurdle to the communication of meaning in a work of art. Viewers trip on the fact that the medium is not paint (or whatever else their biases lead them to expect), then can't get beyond the wonder of the artwork's accomplishment, or the embarrassment of its faults. The medium is so remarkable that it becomes the only message, and other ideas are lost. Realizing this increased my frustration. I rejected tapestry and took up paint, only to return when I had nothing to show for my hours at the easel; at least my time at the loom got results. Still, doubts kept me from the loom like a writer's block. Taking an argument and making an actual physical embodiment of it was all I could do to keep from being completely stymied by it.

Abandoning tapestry for good in my recent work, I've given free rein to my love of structure, materials and ordinary objects as metaphors for larger concerns. While present in my tapestry work, these aspects assume new prominence in pieces such as *Three Ways* and *Bread Cage*. Bread is a timeless symbol, as in nourishment, money, the body of Christ. Classic American white bread connotes homogeneity, conformity and the "Wonder® Bread" era of my childhood. Wrapping it in baling wire is an act of binding, an attempt to restrain it, to better grasp its meaning. But just as barricade tape doesn't physically restrain anyone, wire can't really contain the bread. The slices are dry and brittle. Chunks keep crumbling off.

I'm still wrestling with ideas of confinement and propriety. Lately, I've begun to see them in a spiritual context, juxtaposing the confines of life with the freedom and release of the spirit in death. Unfettered by the demands of tapestry, I work as freely as I can. In my working process I explore a sense of confinement. The work retains a textile nature without being defined by it. Some days my work is a spiritual quest; other days it is an intellectual journey. It's not about producing a product. What you see is a souvenir: evidence of the process.

I'm still wrestling with ideas of confinement and propriety. Lately, I've begun to see them in a spiritual context, juxtaposing the confines of life with the freedom and release of the spirit in death. Some days my work is a spiritual quest. Other days it is an intellectual journey. What you see is a souvenir: evidence of the process.

Bread Cage (1999)
mixed media, wire
12.5 x 12.5 x 23.75cm (5 x 5 x 9½")

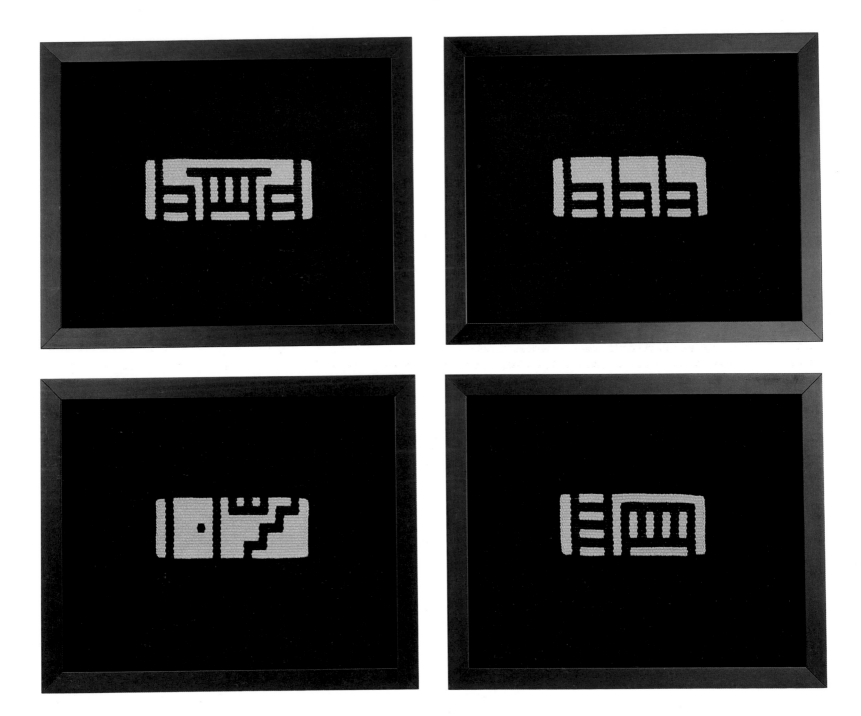

I love the structural qualities of tapestry: the discrete point of weft over warp, the separation of one shape from another, the real, physical edge of a slit...With the simplified iconography of signs these tiny tableaux warn of household hazards or illustrate a domestic rule of order.

Born   1957, Ann Arbor, Michigan

Education and Awards

1975-78	BSE (*summa cum laude*), Computer Engineering, University of Michigan, Ann Arbor, Michigan
1984-88	BFA, Drawing, Pacific Northwest College of Art, Portland, Oregon
1985-88	Scholastic awards (eight), Pacific Northwest College of Art, Portland, Oregon
1989	Award in Fibers, 9th Annual NW International Art Competition, Whatcom Museum of History and Art, Bellingham, Washington

Selected Exhibitions

2000	*Bread,* L & B Viewing Room, Portland, Oregon (solo)
1999	*The Notebook: The Art of the Idea,* L & B Viewing Room, Portland, Oregon
1998	*Fiber National '88,* Adams Memorial Gallery, Dunkirk, New York
1998	*Pacific Northwest College of Art Thesis Exhibition,* Portland Art Museum, Portlnad, Oregon
1996	*Seeking Security: The Human Spirit and the Compulsion to Control,* WORKS/San Jose, California
1996	*Audrey Moore & Linda Hutchins: Tapestries,* Waterstone Gallery, Portland, Oregon
1996	*Passages: Tapestries of the Northwest,* Oregon History Center, Portland, Oregon
1994	*National Tapestry Invitational Exhibition,* Art Space/Lima Gallery, Lima, Ohio
1994	*Tapestry Visions,* Minneapolis College of Art and Design, Minneapolis, Minnesota
1993	*Northwest Tapestry 1993,* Nordic Heritage Museum, Seattle, Washington (tour, three cities)
1991	*The Art of Tapestry Invitational Exhibition,* Bush Barn Art Center, Salem, Oregon
1991	Joanne Rapp Gallery/The Hand and The Spirit, Scottsdale, Arizona
1991	Gallery Eight, La Jolla, California
1990	*Risk Factors,* Portland State University Littman Gallery, Portland, Oregon
1990	*Women's Strength: To Be, To See, To Act,* Blackfish Gallery, Portland, Oregon
1989	*Fiberart '89 International,* Pittsburgh Center for the Arts, Pittsburgh, Pennsylvania
1989	*Tapestries and Drawings,* Oregon School of Arts & Crafts Centrum, Portland, Oregon (solo)

Publications

1995	"Tapestry Comes to Ohio", Carol K. Russell, *FIBERARTS,* Summer Issue
1994	Linda Hutchins, "DO NOT CROSS THIS LINE", *ITNET Journal,* Fall Issue
1991	Nancy Orban, ed., *FIBERARTS Design Book Four* (Lark Books)
1990	*The Tapestry Handbook,* Carol K. Russell, (Lark Books)
1990	"A Fine Line: Opening New Doors", Jessica Scarborough, *FIBERARTS,* Sept/Oct Issue
1989	Linda Hutchins, "Today's Tapestry Trends", *FIBERARTS,* Mar/Apr Issue
1988	"New Works: Linda Hutchins", *FIBERARTS,* Nov/Dec Issue

clockwise from top left:

Table and Chairs, Three Chairs Facing Right, Ladder and Crib and **Door and Stairs** (1996)
woven tapestry (cotton)
22.5 x 27cm (9 x 10¾") each

Susan Lordi Marker

That which is carefully wrapped, protected and put away for another time has value even if never touched or looked at again. Just our awareness of its existence is enough reason to save it. My work affirms the need to keep safe that which cannot be touched.

left:
Soulskin: Seeding the Prairie (1999) (detail)
iron, copper, nylon
painted
190 x 102.5 x 5cm (76 x 41 x 2")

right:
Chrysalid (1993)
cotton, synthetic fiber, paper
painted, stitched
60 x 80 x 22.5cm (24 x 32 x 9")

Preservation carries messages about value and rarity. I am curious about that which survives or endures the passage of time, whether by chance or by deliberate and careful conservation. Preserving both the tangible (objects which have been saved) as well as the intangible (storytelling, memories, beliefs, human experiences) is a theme in much of my work. I show this by integrating substantial, physical substances with more tenuous, translucent materials. Objects or images with seemingly little intrinsic value, presented with reverence and care, question our motives of preservation. My work implies that the ordinary can be transformed and deemed worthy of keeping.

I embrace the idea of 'old, but kept' cloth as a metaphorical expression of people's lives. Clearly, cloth can be physical evidence of past experiences and rituals. Fabric that has been handled, washed, ironed and folded repeatedly possesses a quality evocative of human care. The surfaces I create suggest a history of use. Thus, the cloth is, at times, not only the form but the subject matter: cloth and clothing as manifestations of the lives which possessed them.

The idea that the past continues to inform the present intrigues me. In *Manifesto*, a dialogue among generations is glimpsed through a palimpsest of images and text. This layering could imply gradual disappearance, yet also suggest a process of unfolding and emerging.

The intimacy I seek in my pieces depends on engaging the viewer with transformations of surfaces and materials. Touching, making and shaping fiber is an exciting and compelling process, not just a means to an end. I love to take a piece of cloth and push it; make it shrink, then expand, rise up, then recede, become sheer, then opaque. It is a challenge for me to create contrasts, a surface energy or tension the viewer can sense. After all, I work the cloth until it bears the humanness; it must breathe the hand of the maker.

I have always been interested in language and oral traditions of storytelling. It seems that those tales that survive do so because of their surprising relevance to the present. Stories from elderly members of my own family have fuelled much of my work. The text I use is from handwritings of those who have recorded personal stories, proverbs, or life experiences. The writing is photographically transferred by silkscreen so that it retains all of the original character. Early on, I printed text with pigment or dye. Later, I began using a mild acid which etches or burns the original handwriting into the surface of the cloth, integrating it permanently with the structure.

It is not so important that the words are able to be read; rather, that they connote communication beyond the written word. Carefully wrapped in a box in a drawer are some pieces of linen which were hand-woven over 100 years ago by my great-grandmother. I feel a responsibility to save these remnants, not because of their intrinsic value, but because years before I had them, someone else had preserved them. Time goes by and I may never look in that box, yet I know it's there. That which is carefully wrapped, protected and put away for another time has value even if never touched or looked at again. Just our awareness of its existence is enough reason to save it. My work affirms the need to keep safe that which cannot be touched.

I love the vulnerability of cloth. This work is a very fragile, ethereal form that has a body or skin-like reference. Skin, like cloth, is fragile and vulnerable to the elements, and I question what really endures.

Soulskin: Listening to Julia (1995)
linen, silk, cotton
dyed, stitched, devoré
75 x 67.5 x 7.75cm (30 x 27 x 3")

The most precious objects I own are letters from family and friends. In a time when hand-written letters are becoming scarce, I wanted to build a protective space. I began wrapping and stitching string, gauze and sheer silk around stacks of letters. This led to the piece *Chrysalid*. The title refers to the impending emergence from a cocoon. The partially concealed, bundled forms speak about suspended time and our need to preserve the intangible things that we hold close.

In my *Excavation* and *Soulskin* series, I present cloth and clothing as having the same significance as other essential elements of the earth. In this way, I want to elevate the value of cloth as personal evidence of a life. *Soulskin: Listening to Julia* is a very fragile, ethereal form that has a body or skin-like quality. I love the vulnerability that cloth shares with skin.

Discoveries about my own family history have given me a greater understanding of where I stand in the present. I am interested in why certain memories, stories and beliefs survive and are revealed and renewed through time. I try to capture this awareness in the objects that I make.

My most recent work continues to explore the theme of preservation. This past year I bought a piece of land outside the city. I have spent many days and nights immersed in an environment of meadows, woods and lake. I am gradually re-introducing the native prairie grasses and making efforts to preserve and nurture the wildlife.

Time and process take on new meanings; 'readings' of tree skeletons, tracks in the mud, bark patterns, thousands of opening seed heads and the indefatigable patience of the heron are now becoming my text. This new venture has had a profound impact on my work. The excitement of a change in surroundings and the daily observations of decay, rebirth and survival in the wild have opened the floodgates of possibilities.

Manifesto (1993)
cotton
printed, dyed, painted, stitched
162.5 x 162.5 x 12.5cm (65 x 65 x 5")

**I work the cloth until it bears the humanness;
it must breathe the hand of the maker.**

Here I present cloth as having the same significance as other essential elements of the earth. Much of the linen is burnt away, leaving a thin, transparent veil of fiber connecting what remains.

Extending the piece 13" away from the wall gives it a floating, tenuous presence. I wanted to elevate the value of cloth as personal evidence of a life.

Excavation: Soulskin #11 (1997)
linen blend
dyed, painted, cloqué, devoré
165 x 85cm (66 x 34")

Born   1954, Beaver Falls, Pennsylvania

Education and Awards

1972-76	Bachelor of Science (Honors), University of Missouri, Columbia
1990-93	Graduate Merit and Research Awards (four), University of Kansas, Lawrence, Kansas
1990-93	Master of Fine Arts (Honors), University of Kansas, Lawrence, Kansas
1991	Second Prize, *Fiberart International,* Pittsburgh, Pennsylvania
1992	Jurors' Choice Award, *Fiber Directions,* Wichita, Kansas
1993	Jurors' Choice Award, *Fiberart International,* Pittsburgh, Pennsylvania
1994	Special Mention Award, *Biennial International Textile Design Contest,* Tokyo, Japan
1998	Best of Show Award, *Muse of the Millennium: Emerging Trends in Fiber Art,* Seattle, Washington

Selected Exhibitions

2000	*Material Evidence,* Reed Whipple Center, Las Vegas, Nevada (tour)
2000	*Measure for Measure,* H & R Bloch Artspace, Kansas City, Missouri
1999	*Past as Prologue,* The Society for Contemporary Crafts, Pittsburgh, Pennsylvania (four persons)
1999	*Beneath the Surface: Artist's Dropcloths,* Center of Contemporary Arts (COCA), St.Louis, Missouri
1999	*Rising to the Surface,* Southern Oregon University, Ashland, Oregon
1998	*Muse of the Millennium: Emerging Trends in Fiber Art,* Nordic Heritage Museum, Seattle, Washington
1996-98	*Transcending the Surface,* Hunterdon Museum of Art, Clinton, New Jersey (tour, five cities)
1997	*Surface Tension: New Works in Textiles,* Center of Contemporary Arts (COCA), St. Louis, Missouri
1995-96	*Textile as Narrative/Ritual,* ARC Gallery, Chicago, Illinois (tour)
1995	*New Tools,* Littman and White Gallery, Portland, Oregon
1994	*Biennial International Textile Design Contest,* Tokyo, Japan
1994	*Susan Lordi Marker,* Appalachian Center for Crafts, Smithville, Tennessee (solo)
1993, 94	*Chautauqua International for Fiber Art,* Dunkirk, New York
1993	*Susan Lordi Marker: Resonant Voices,* University of Kansas Art and Design Gallery, Lawrence, Kansas (solo)
1993	*Unspoken Dialogues: Fiber Constructions,* Regents Center, Overland Park, Kansas (solo)
1993	*Artists and Language,* The Society for Contemporary Crafts, Pittsburgh, Pennsylvania
1991, 93	*Fiberart International Biennial,* Pittsburgh Center for the Arts, Pennsylvania

Publications

1999	"Susan Lordi Marker: Explorations in Cloth", Michele Fricke, *Surface Design Journal* vol.23, no.2
1994	"Susan Lordi Marker: Resonant Voices", *Surface Design Journal* vol.18, no.3

Professional

1998-	Instructor, Fiber, Kansas City Art Institute, Kansas City, Missouri
1993-96	Lecturer, Design, University of Kansas, Lawrence, Kansas

Other specialist textile publications from Telos Art Publishing

Art Textiles of the World

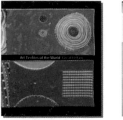 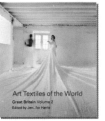  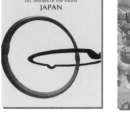 

Art Textiles of the World: Great Britain Volume 1
Edited by Matthew Koumis, introduction by Amanda Fielding

Jeanette Appleton, Jo Barker, Kate Blee, Sara Brennan,
Dawn Dupree, Sally Greaves-Lord, Nicola Henley,
Greg Parsons, Marta Rogoyska, Lynn Setterington
ISBN: 0 9526267 2 1
112pp • softback • 103 col. illus. • 286 x 244mm • £25

Art Textiles of the World: Great Britain Volume 2
Edited with an introduction by Dr Jennifer Harris

Rushton Aust, Polly Binns, Michael Brennand-Wood,
Caroline Broadhead, Jo Budd, Sally Freshwater, Shelly Goldsmith,
Alice Kettle, Janet Ledsham, Lesley Mitchison
ISBN: 0 9526267 6 4
96pp • softback • 52 col. Illus. • 286 x 242mm • £25

Art Textiles of the World: Japan
Edited by Matthew Koumis, introduction by Keiko Kawashima

Machiko Agano, Masae Bamba, Yasuko Fujino, Masashi Honda,
Haruko Honma, Masakazu & Naomi Kobayashi, Kiyonori
Shimada, Hiroyuki Shindo, Yuko Takada, Chiyoko Tanaka,
Mitsuo Toyazaki, Chiyu Uemae
ISBN: 0 9526267 4 8
128pp • softback • 118 col. illus. • 286 x 242mm • £25

Art Textiles of the World: Australia
Edited by Matthew Koumis, introduction by Sue Rowley

Awely Utopia Batik Aboriginal Community, Patricia Black,
Elena Gallegos, Pam Gaunt, Ruth Hadlow, Jan Irvine,
Elsje van Keppel, Valerie Kirk, Tori de Mestre, Patrick Snelling
ISBN: 0 9526267 0 5
96pp • softback • 52 col. illus. • 286 x 242mm • £25

Art Textiles of the World: The Netherlands (Oct 2001)
Edited with an introduction by Dery Timmer

Marijke Arp, Marian Bijlenga, Sonja Besselink, Hil Driessen,
Maryan Geluk, Ella Koopman, Wilma Kuil, Nel Linssen,
Karola Pezarro, Marian Smit
ISBN: 1 902015 00 2
96pp • softback • 52 col. illus. • 286 x 242mm • £25

Reinventing Textiles

**A forum for critical debate, with cutting-edge essays
by leading writers, artists and curators around the world**

Reinventing Textiles
VOL. 1: TRADITION & INNOVATION
Edited by Sue Rowley

Volume 1: Tradition & Innovation
Edited with an introduction by Professor Sue Rowley

Essays by Julian Ruesga Bono, Hazel Clark,
Diana Wood Conroy, Wlodzimierz Cygan,
Jasleen Dhamija, Janis Jefferies, Doreen Mellor,
Margo Mensing, Nima Poovaya-Smith

ISBN: 1 902015 0 2

168 pp • softback • 15col. & 10 b&w illus.
230 x 160mm • £19.95

Volume 2: Gender and the Body (October 2001)
Edited with an introduction by Janis Jefferies , ISBN: 1 902015 10 X

Essays by Renée Baert, Alison Ferris, Peter Hobbs, Barbara Layne, Victoria Lynne
with Nailini Malai, Sarat Maharaj, Lindsay Obermeyer with Kay Lawrence,
Tina Sherwell, Kim Sung-Jung, Lisbeth Tolstrup, Giorgia Volpe with Mariette Bouillet

Volume 3: The Politics of Curatorship (October 2002)
Edited with an introduction by Dr Jennifer Harris, ISBN: 1 902015 11 8

Portfolio Series

**Monographs of outstanding artists
working across a broad spectrum of textiles**
Texts in English, Dutch and Japanese

Jilly Edwards
ISBN: 1 902015 20 7
48pp • 20 col. illus. • 220 x 220mm • £12.50
Foreword by Lene Bragger
Texts by Melanie Cook

Marian Bijlenga
ISBN: 1 902015 21 5
48pp • 20 col. illus. • 220 x 220mm • £12.50
Foreword by Jack Lenor Larsen
Text by Gert Staal

For further details, please visit our website: **www.arttextiles.com**